What others are saying about *The Oracle Teachings*:

"The Oracle provides new insights and a unique framework for unlocking the soul's potential for giving and receiving love in an otherwise turbulent world. Remarkable, inspiring, and highly readable!"

- Eric P. Gruendemann, Producer "HERCULES - The Legendary Journeys" and "ZENA - Warrior Princess" Television Series

"Open this book to any page and you will find the wisdom you are seeking; precise answers for your asking. The Oracle is a master teacher of divine wisdom who opens the way for each of us to claim our own modern wisdom. She teaches that we are not here to save our souls. Rather our souls are here to save us and to lead us back to divine love."

- M. C. Breckenridge, Trustee, *Lightworks Unlimited*

"'For I will not give you answers. I will propel you into your own destiny of purification and wholeness and the answers that shall come.' So begins the latest expression of The Oracle: *The Oracle Teachings, Soul Over Mind*. Reading this book is a process in and of itself. There are Teachings about love and humanity's origins in love, and also the removal of false premises which keep the mind locked away from the soul. In *The Oracle Teachings* the reader moves towards enlightenment through understanding the deeper structures of reality and encountering the truth about salvation, evolution, choice and faith. There are also beautiful meditations and illustrative case histories about the Oracle Teachings. A sure hit for all new thought readers."

- *Leading Edge Review*

"Oracle shines a golden light on us as we read her book. She shows how we can see the goddess or god inside ourselves and the path towards letting our wonderment shine on others every day."

- Kare Anderson, author of *Beauty Inside Out*

"Neptune conjuncts Mercury in The Oracle's 7th house, designating her as a visionary messenger endowed with special gifts and the ability to receive images and wisdom holographically. Saturn also conjuncts Mercury in The Oracle's natal chart, denoting that she maintains clear focus and is precise and disciplined. Notables who share these conjunctions are Albert Einstein, Dr. Martin Luther King Jr., Edgar Cayce, Jeanne Dixon, Joan Grant, Frederic Chopin and Nikola Tesla."
- Joyce Timmons Coit, *Master Astrologer, Hawai'i*

"Reading The Oracle's book reawakens my heart and soul to the divine love. In fact, it seems as if my heart took wings. I feel a greater understanding and compassion for all living beings including myself. What a gift of divine wisdom. The book touched me more deeply than books by Leo Buscaglia and brought me more joy than Deepak Chopra. The Oracle has been a source of total inspiration as I open myself to divine love."
- Reverend Marci Ross, *Transformational Bodyworker*

"In her writing, Oracle offers a vision of our own self as someone worth knowing, a home worth coming home to. She provides a path that asks nothing more of us than the effort it takes on a hot sunny day to drink a cold glass of our favorite herb tea. If you like the thought of relaxing, cuddling, wallowing in the pure joy of being alive, you are going to love Oracle's approach to the metaphysical issues of our time. If you are a quote collector, get out your pencil and paper."
- Jacqueline Levy, *Levy Communications*

"Life's 'big' questions are answered simply and clearly in this fantastic new release. The Oracle cuts through confusing and debilitating myth that has plagued those attempting to live life on the 'spiritual path'.

"This book offers practical and effective ways to purify oneself and release blockages that bar one from a full return to the Self."
- Paul W. Dennis, *Manager, Quest Distributors*

THE ORACLE SERIES BOOK II

The
Oracle Teachings

Soul Over Mind

The Oracle

ORACLE PRODUCTIONS LTD
Kaua'i, Hawai'i   Auckland, New Zealand

The Oracle Series:
The Oracle Speaks: Breakthroughs for Humanity I
The Oracle Teachings: Soul Over Mind II
Meditate With The Oracle **Cassettes**

The Oracle Teachings: Soul Over Mind
The Oracle Series Book II
Copyright © 1996 by The Oracle. Published by Oracle Productions Ltd.
P. O. Box 3300-393, Princeville, Kaua'i, HI 96722-3300 U.S.A E-mail: oracleprod@aol.com
First printing 1996.

Library of Congress Catalog Card Number: 96-67000

ISBN 0-9648443-3-8: U.S. $14.75, AUS$28.75, NZ$32.75

Publisher's Cataloging in Publication

Oracle.
   The Oracle teachings: soul over mind / the Oracle.
   p. cm. — (Oracle series ; no. 2)
   ISBN 0-9648443-3-8

   1. Self-actualization. 2. Self-realization. 3. Ethics. I. Title. II. Title: Soul over mind.

BF637.S4073 1996   171.3
                                     QBI96-20076
Cover design: Melanie Friedfeld, Hawai'i
Final editing: Christine Young, New Zealand

CONTENTS

I personally welcome you to be still and open to receive the wondrous divine love essence that is a natural part of ourselves. My journey has been a sacred evolution into purer states of consciousness. I share this divine expression with you and bless your journey into wholeness. The direct path is the shortest one.

ORACLE

INTRODUCTION

In her teachings The Oracle says, "We have come from love for love. Lay down your differences and pick up the wonders of the universe. Display them and herald the voice of peace and truth."

The Oracle Teachings: Soul Over Mind is a profound book of new thinking, oraculars, and personal experiences to assist humanity in its search for love, knowledge and truth. The inclusion of an insightful chapter of false premises powerfully builds upon previously exposed false beliefs in the first book of The Oracle Series, *The Oracle Speaks: Breakthroughs for Humanity.*

Several individual case studies, derived from private intensive sessions with The Oracle are shared. These give an inside look into how the direct experience of divine love creates transformation and opens one to amazing new possibilities. Empowerment techniques used to unveil the soul of the being are shared for your benefit. The enlightenment and insights that the participants obtained from their personally guided Oracle Teachings propelled each one into major advances of self-knowledge, purification and experiences of love.

"The universal divine love light embraces us all with energy. It is up to us to release ourselves into its pure ecstasy and joy. Allow yourself to join in the celebration of being in the place of the universe's divine love. It is for you to partake and to bless those around you. Drink from this well of holy nectar and anoint your family and friends with the essence."

CHAPTER ONE

THE   BEGINNING

In the beginning you were loved, blessed and graced by the universe. If you could see where you were in your beginning, you would be able to see that you were a sacred energy being whose soul emitted and received universal divine love and holy light. You would see yourself as a part of all life and of everything. The sensation would be profound and endless. You would know all and express by thought and love energy without time or linear thinking. This is who and what you are naturally. *Through interactive divine love meditation you can remember and recall this for yourself, now.*

I have come to share the knowledge of the divine existence. It begins with your willingness to observe and inquire into the deepest secrets of your past. *For I will not give you answers. I will propel you into your own destiny of purification and wholeness and the answers that shall come.*

You want to feel complete and free. You want to access at will all that there is. You want to develop your inner senses and skills in order to provide for yourself and those around you. This all can be and will be, for you are returning to your beginning.

The way to the beginning is to undo, unlearn and erase all that the mind has contrived into a complicated enmeshment of false ideas. These ideas perpetuate a faulty matrix pattern that defaults one away from soul oneness and its love. Each time you speak, act and live from untrue mind-based ideas, you will distance yourself from love and further suppress your soul. It has become a common practice for humans to express limited ideas in place of love expression. So much so, that the majority have become lost in it.

Overall, the spiritual journey will only have entailed the release of the mental harnessing and constraints that have been used to limit one's identity and self-expression. This release is called soul over mind. You will eventually find yourself at the beginning. When you are there, it will feel like the beginning, and you will have remembrance of the journey you have taken to arrive there once again.

You will have the sensation of awareness for all that is expressed in love. *You will see that you always have been and there was no beginning and there is no end; only a journey to understand.* It is a very secure existence for the ones who see and re-experience their true selves. The full circle of the journey to self-realization will be achieved, and then an opportunity arises to describe the accomplishment and assist others to theirs. *Once the release of your past is complete, it will leave a purified being with a fully unveiled soul. This is soul over mind.*

The soul nurtured by its return to wholeness spreads the light and speaks inside your heart and your head. You, the real soul-self you, with confidence and wisdom becomes fully revealed. The past will seem like a ride on a mental highway of drugged and intoxicated unserving experiences perpetuated by mass media, over-population and unsophisticated behavior standards. You will celebrate and rejoice in the freedom of being your purified self; a being of love in embodiment with individual personality. Caress yourself with the universe's waves of love and dance in delight as the inner natural nectars of the glands are allowed to function in optimum healthiness.

You are now able to choose the course that takes you into your self awareness. Done well, you will not get lost in the tunnel of transformation, and will walk through it to be fully into the light. Do not get lost in a particular practice, method or ideology. It will only hinder your growth. It is better to surrender to your soul's guidance. Your soul will lead you and speak to you. *It is that occasional, soft, reliable and truthful inner voice that you hear from deep inside. The soul when in full communication can be heard.* When listened to it always includes the best outcome for everyone. Only the mind eliminates and conceals the soul's existence. Only the mind divides you from the sacred light and its oneness. Do not settle for mind over soul living.

Imagine for a moment that you are standing along the shoreline of a beautiful crystal blue lake that has been warmed by the sun. You are only a few feet away from the water. As you begin to meditate, you move your body into the sacred water and become engulfed by its energy and being. You feel embraced by its wondrous healing properties and feel relaxed in the fluid calmness it contains. This is what the soul is like.

The mind, storing words and information in the brain, separates you from the soul and pulls you out of the wholeness of the lake of love. If you can return to the lake and swim and play in its grace, you can return to your soul in oneness with the universe's oversoul. This experience has been called enlightenment, God, holy trinity, unity or Christ consciousness, divine love, nirvana, samadhi, emptiness, cosmic consciousness, bliss, sati-supreme reality, etc. The wellspring of the oversoul grants all to the individual soul, and you are embraced with love and its truth and wisdom. You can then always communicate freely with it to receive the necessary knowledge for personal guidance. *You need only ask in a sincere manner and the universe replies with love.* It is the easiest way to live and you no longer have the stress and added energy diversion of trying to hold yourself together in separation along the shoreline.

When one surrenders the ego, the opportunity to join the oneness of the universe is taken. You then benefit from the support and power of the entire universe rather than trying to create in a separate and singular manner. Do you see how powerful it is to give up trying to make it on your own? Instead, you can receive your inheritance of the entire flow of the universe's love and guidance. Is it so hard to surrender the mind's ego to have it all?

Walk into your divinity and rediscover yourself. You will be caressed in pure love and see the secrets of the universe that have never been secret. The divine love light will then be heard by you and will co-create with your soul, the life you always dreamed you could have.

The Oracle Teachings are comprised of five basic, profound teachings designed to purify and evolve the soul, so it may fully blossom. Each transformation is a valuable gem to gain, as is letting go of the valueless, distorted fears of your past. The place to begin is at the end, where you may presently find yourself. The sacred light will guide you back to the beginning using these five precious teachings that will generate wholeness, wellness and freedom. It is time for you to address your needs and reveal your soul memory in order to release the holdings of limited consciousness in exchange for unlimited beingness.

This book will show in detail the five Oracle Teachings that truly progress people. This will be done by sharing intensive, one on one personal sessions between The Oracle and individuals who were willing to have their experiences published for your benefit and understanding. At times they did not know they were in a veil and it was hard work to break through the hidden barrier they had unconsciously built. Once the enlightenment occurred, they could see they were shielding themselves and were not in their power nor their true identity.

Sometimes it is a very tricky game that the mind and its ego plays on the self. It is stimulating to withdraw from its grasp, unraveling the ties into love and holiness. *The ecstasy of truth and love is what I am here to impart. For the way it is, is the way it has always been and the way it will be. You will see your soul-self for the first time anew and renewed in the supreme nobility of universal divinity.*

Before The Oracle Teachings are presented to a group of people, the group is asked to have an inner conversation. The conversation is an authentic asking of the mind to surrender to the soul for the Oracle session. This prepares the mind to begin to yield to the guidance that the soul will provide during the program presentation. The person then has compliance from the mind to allow the soul to speak. It is thereby heard by the individual and the individual can process what is revealed. Through inner requests of asking the mind to relax, it will soften and let the soul surface and integrate on a conscious level.

It is through the re-integration process, using the five profound teachings, that one becomes clear and aligned with the soul. That is the reason for the process and the outcome of the process. The teachings are easy, simple and for everyone to use at any time. They are not strict, strange or strenuous. They are distinct and powerful and bring immediate results of advancement. *It is not a searching for experience, it is rather a shedding to remember one's self experience.* By removing the layers of the mind, you will unveil the radiance of the soul, and shine brightly with your love into the world and unto yourself. It is the greatest and most rewarding treatment of oneself to journey into the realms of your personal history. *You will never forget the revelations of the soul, yet you will forgive the tribulations of the mind.*

Be open to the possibilities of the self you restrain within. Start having conversations with yourself to build your confidence. See your hidden secrets and the false ideas that inhibit your expression of your life purpose and desires. From experience, I find people are functioning, on the average, with five to 20 major false distinctions in their mind which have been created from weak thinking. Some have only one to four major blocks. The number isn't important. *What is important is the intensity and hold that each false distinction carries.* These false distinctions are not in alignment with your identity or the laws of the universe.

Let yourself commence the steps backward to your beginning, one at a time, to see who and what you really are. Discard your protective identity for your profound self and stand tall in the love of the universe. You will

beam and be comforted forevermore in the grace of all
that there is, and only what there is.

CHAPTER TWO

FALSE PREMISES

Before the teachings are presented, there are false premises to be unmasked. This is important in order to prepare you for the onward adventure into your divine consciousness. *If you hold onto false premises expounded by inauthentic authorities and your own mind, you will be forsaking your profound and holy vibration to untrue statements. Why base one's life on such unreal ideas?* They will only inhibit your progress and starve your heart.

False premises are strongly believed in by members of various structures, organizations, institutions, clubs, societies, chapters, orders, synagogues, churches, temples and cults. They base their existence upon their code, dogma, history, rituals and perpetuation of their control and influence. The exchange between member and hierarchy, although misidentified, is an equal one, always in balance. In other words, the leader and the follower have chosen their roles and corresponding dynamics. Only the groupings that are based in purity are clear, useful and rewarding for they operate without false premises.

I am not speaking of perfection, only how perfectly our universe balances every thought and resulting action. What is not known is that each and every falsely premised thought and action results in your hindering forward progress. Each and every one of them adds to, enmeshes and exponentially grows with the others. This decline in human consciousness dilutes the ability of the species to birth geniuses and leaders. Layer upon layer of cultures and schools which, separate themselves from the central energy and laws of the universe, are reinforced electronically, visually, and psychically. It is for this reason that it is such an accomplished feat, a mastery, for a human to become an enlightened one, one of wisdom, one of philosophy, one to bear the light.

It is not loving for humanity to bury, hide and place veils upon the soul. Through personal responsibility you have the inner skill to unveil your soul and discard the many false premises that have been taught to you. Soul over mind living is your passage into ecstasy and sanity.

Can you perceive what a few false premises may be? The following are a few of the most predominant among those which carry a lot of weight. May the wisdom not challenge; instead may it lift your spirit and free your soul.

May you begin to experience soul over mind.

FALSE PREMISE

My language and expressions are not universal
tools of creation.

Contrary to society's practice, the misuse of language and the everyday allowance of harmful, racist and violent thoughts greatly inhibit our evolution. When operating in a state of mind over soul, humanity becomes loose, sloppy and mean in its speaking and inner thoughts; *not realizing that each word has a presence and commanding force which is taken as an order by the universe.*

Certain pockets of human population may be so-called civilized. The question is, are they really "advanced"? Is humankind fooling itself by believing that it is advanced because of technology, capitalism and democracy? Take a moment to observe the world society and your local community. How are people treating each other? How are people speaking to each other? How are people working together? What is being hidden from the people? How are the people being used? Is censorship occurring? Is violence increasing? Is health purchased, or equal to all?

Is there racism of color, creed, religion, class, gender, age, education, weight, height, location, financial stature, etc.? Why does society have the following words expressed daily in all media: murder, rape or date-rape, kidnap, beaten, abused, assassinated, criminal, convict, poverty, starvation, welfare, bulimia, anorexia, addiction, stress, mental illness, deprivation, kill, armed guard, military forces, bombs, bullets, guns, rifles, grenades, star wars, secret service, undercover agents, militia, swat teams, police, prowler, self-defense, ammunition, boot camp, invasion, atrocities, slavery, demolish, genocide, holocaust, war, demilitarized zone, cease-fire, rip-off, lies, cheating, stealing, conning, sting, distrustful, shrewd, prison, concentration camp, burglar, burglary, theft, arsonist, betrayal, weapons, espionage, spy, culprit, gossip, naysayer, hate, cruelty, evil, devil, crucifixion, jail, terrorism, codependency, sadist, masochist, dysfunctional, insane, dominate, blacklists, sorry, apologize, guilt, shame, anger, meanness, conspiracy, and Mafia?

Language carries use, meaning, intention, description, and communication. There are many more words that are discriminatory in their reference to skin color, culture and gender. Why are such words as these in our language and in daily occurrence? Why is there a perpetuation of these words in our language? Why do they dominate the media? Humanity does not know that its very own words are creating and perpetuating such a society. Humanity does not know its soul-self. Why does humanity continue to tread upon itself?

When one becomes holy, only goodness is spoken. The actions that follow the good words demonstrate congenial living. Stop for a moment and listen to your present inner thoughts and your previous thoughts of the past week. Review what you have heard and seen in the media. If you eliminate all negative wording and the thoughts behind them, what wording and thoughts would you be left with?

What if you filled the new space with more of the positive and empowering words? Words such as love, friendship, beauty, sharing, caressing, nurturing, supportive, peacefulness, relaxation, kindness, compassion, serenity, wisdom, knowledge, beloved, holy, divinity, achievement, accomplishment, joy, sacred, harmony, wholeness, happiness, support, contribution, assistance, as well as artistic words of expression and fulfillment, and language that is healing. Imagine if all that you heard and spoke each day was positive and uplifting? Would life not be different? Would you not be different?

Is there power in our choice of words? Why do some cultures not have a word for artist? Is it because everyone was an artist? Why do some cultures not have separate words for mind, soul and consciousness? Is it because they look at the person as a "whole" being? What new words of endearment can be added to our language? Does language need word opposites to exist? No, love can exist without hate, good can exist without bad, freedom can exist without confinement, suppression and oppression. The divine light exists without all negatives - even evil or hell. These are human-made concepts and levels of consciousness that dominate the masses. *The universe is made of sound, light and consciousness. It vibrates in pure love.*

All that you think, visualize, feel and do is a real force moving out into the universe, creating your world and your participation with the world. Your expression inward or outward effects everything everywhere. *Is it not time to understand that you are your words and that you control your destiny by your words?* Do not take your words lightly. Do create light with them as they are the most tremendously effective universal tools. They are your colors to paint on the blank canvas of life. It is time for your divine artistry to unfold. Give your thoughts, your speaking and those of others the honor they deserve. Your life will change and the universe will bring new feedback that is from and for the glory of your soul. See how easily you can paint your true masterpiece.

FALSE PREMISE

*Each incarnation I will become purer, more
evolved and a step closer to enlightenment.*

It is not a linear pattern. It is not a reverse pattern. It is
not a mixed pattern. There exists only you and your
soul. *There exists only your inner thoughts and the
access to the creative space that exists before thought and
vision.*

As you begin to review your personal soul history
through interactive divine love meditation, you will start
to see where and what you have been. You will recall the
strongest thoughts, ideas and distinctions both true and
false. For your own evolution you can recall those that
are erroneous and be given the opportunity to learn from
them. Likewise you can review the true ones and be
empowered by them. Each contains gifts of wisdom that
are stored in your soul memory.

The predominant path of most people's incarnations is to
repeat limiting cycles based upon multiple misinterpretations or unreal conclusions. As they build and

amass these misinterpretations through each lifetime, a more complex situation is created that is difficult to unravel without reaching deep into one's soul memory. Introspection and purification are not often used in previous experiences. Mostly, a person will begin from original emergence with a limiting barrier and carry it through to the present existence; along the way adding more instances of hurt, betrayal, abandonment, pain, suffering, and enduring.

With a compounded soul history of inauthentic patterning it gets more and more complicated to undo, unlearn, and clear the many false distinctions. This is compounded by the fact that one adds to them from occurrences in the current life. On the whole, in other words, humanity is downgrading itself continuously.

In each life you have made poor and weak choices which shape your current experiences and those that will follow. With your choices based upon fear, anger, hurt, or a lack of any kind, you will repeat the pattern. As each moment is the time of choice, you have had many moments creating who you are today, most often choosing from unknown false ideas buried deeply in your consciousness.

Some incarnations were easier than others. Each was based upon a need or desire to achieve what your internal dialogue was fueling. Each added causal negative patterning. Usually the more incarnations, the more blocks to enlightenment are created. As your inner dialogue changes from impure to pure and from pure to impure, your life is run not as a linear experience but a random one. The randomness is due only to your choices. Your experience is truly what you have chosen from moment to moment; thoughts that are impure or pure, each an order you command of interaction with your soul or mind. That is all.

It is not enough to be a good citizen, a good family person and a good worker. Mere attendance at religious or spiritual services does not bring one closer to purity. The increasing of one's inner light is the way to purity according to universal law. Be careful each day not to grow further into the unclarity. Learn to trust yourself to see your past and relax into the divine messages that will be released as you replace the impure thoughts with truth. *Build your determination and persevere to cleanse your mind and allow it to surrender to your soul.*

To purify and be enlightened is to erase what is untrue from your "entire past". As you dissolve the erroneous distinctions and their reflective symptoms you will begin to drive your life with truths of the universe. Reverse and retrieve yourself from deep within. The resulting transformations will bring you out of linear thinking and linear goals in to divine love and holy insight, into the universe that dwells in its sacred vibration and function. You can dwell there too.

Know that what you clear today will not hinder your tomorrow, yet if your choices of tomorrow are poor, you will hinder your days thereafter. Be careful; each word and thought holds power in the universe to manifest itself. You have a choice. It is truly up to you to empower yourself by emitting love and truth or to disempower yourself by repeating negative past experiences in your current living.

FALSE PREMISE

Our lives are pre-determined and all we can do is act them out. I am not creating these experiences; they are happening to me.

People don't know that "they are making up" the entire context from which they live. You are cause in the matter of every experience, interaction and thought. As you grow and develop soul over mind, you begin to see, feel, and hear from the profound place of consciousness that exists before words and thoughts. You also build an independent skill of creating clear, universally aligned interpretations of life messages, experiences and communications. Life, when lived in the present and in a state of divine love presence, occurs as a serene and joyfully smooth lifestyle. Each experience is seen clearly for what it is, along with a positive interpretation that reinforces holy principles.

People think certain thoughts and interpret certain experiences to mean something when they are actually meaningless. They then operate from the domain of these thoughts and ideas. Humans are constantly in the state of comparing and judging oneself and others. If you were to stand aside from this type of thought patterning, you would be able to observe life. Taking the time to become the observer gives you the space to create better interpretations of what is happening in your life and in the lives of those around you.

People do not know that they are cause in all matters of their life; cause originating from their own inner thought and not from the external world - and certainly not a pre-determined one. The universe does not do to you. Others do not do to you. You do unto yourself and manifest all of that which is reflected in your life. If you can grasp this one universal law, you will release yourself from a subjective experience, an enduring experience and a victim lifestyle.

Additionally, you are at cause, which includes being responsible for the upliftment of and caring for those around you. You can assist them to meet their commitments to you, as well. If they are not effective individually, it is your additional responsibility to remind them of their promises so that they can follow through. In the sweet presence of your reminder conversation, they will not fail; they will learn of completion and performance. Then everyone is happy.

You are the driving source for all that you experience. Do not sit back and watch yourself or others fail. You can mentor and model ownership of a supreme reality. The trend and results you create will be solely based upon what you truly need and desire inside. That is why I say it is so important to hear your soul's message. *Your soul is beckoning with reason and knowledge to bail you out of your past. It will override the mind and place you in the wonders of divine flow. It will support you in originating the will and design of your life from the central source of the all empowering energy of universal divine love consciousness. If you want to attend any institution of higher learning, join the soul university.*

Having the knowledge that you are the only creator of your life's experiences returns the responsibility to yourself, and you no longer need to rely upon what may come your way today. Instead, you parent and birth each step of your growth and success. You can obtain great leaps of accomplishment and consciousness advancement through this natural and honorable way of progressing. *We are here to care and love, not to suppress and survive.* Please give yourself permission to emerge from your comfort zone of hiding from your identity and gifts, into the wondrous expression of all that you are! It is easier to let go and blossom and flourish from your inner light. Your life is there to create, not wait. Your life is there to design, not resign. Your life is there as an expression of your present determination.

FALSE PREMISE

Trusting and hoping that it will all get better and humanity, as a whole, will evolve one day.

With the combined limitations that false premises have woven, the planetary environment will be completely destroyed and become unable to support human life. The amount of time it would take to enlighten each individual human, a population of 12 billion in 52 years, is beyond reasonable measure. During the next 52 years and on and on, the topsoil, rain forests, food supplies, clean fresh water, atmosphere, other creature contributions, and elements necessary to sustain life, will continue to be polluted, raped, made extinct, bombed, excavated, and destroyed by radiation, chemicals, trampling, and other abominable activities directed by humankind.

The collective ego is led to believe that the ecological status of the planet is improving. It is like sticking one's head in the ground and thinking it is safe. Our ecological balance is so overboard and past the point of return, that it is too much for many to face. Looking the other way is apathetic and drop-out behavior. How much of the world population is educated to understand the extent of the planet's status today? Even the most educated do not know all of it. What they do know is horrific when combined into an overall state of affairs report.

Humanity has been tampering with, using, manipulating and destroying the natural environment for a long time. Additionally, our predecessors have developed civilizations that have become dependent on the very materials and devices that harm the planet, other species and ourselves. We not only need spiritual enlightenment, we need planetary enlightenment and monetary enlightenment. It is an economic, financial and capitalistic racism that is thwarting the survival of all that we know. It is very dark to place these non-universal law based principles onto our new generations and the existing world population.

Let go of your hope and hiding that it will all get better one day. It is not better today. It is worse and getting worse. Where you can make the most positive change is to become enlightened and function from the core of love, compassion and kindness. Then and only then, will you be all that you can be. Then and only then, will you model the universal consciousness. Humankind is still in the dark ages of the mind. You can be responsible for your own life and its outcome. Your passage into this realization will propel you from where you have been into the divine essence that feeds us all. It is up to you, not "they" or "them". There are too many who are still increasing and enmeshing their negative pasts. Go beyond their level and claim your destiny - the life of soulfulness.

FALSE PREMISE

The "second coming" will save us all.

If the universe is and always was a supreme reality vibrating in a constant state of love and ecstasy, why is it that certain humans believe so many billions of years later, one or two people will save us all; save us from what and in what way?

Is it not a put-down to previous others, that the so-called first coming only took place two thousand years ago? In a universe that is timeless and endless, what short existence of a human has that much weight when related to or compared to the entire universe?

If you buy into the belief that you will be saved only through another and most clearly, only one certain other, you will have subordinated yourself to an invented idea made to control and use the masses. *True spirituality and holiness is based on the upliftment of each soul,* not the lowering by indoctrination of all others left to search for godliness and to worship and idolize an ancient human being and the organizations structured around these concepts. True prophets are true teachers, even though so-called "ordained" others have censored their contribution for survival in their self-created hierarchy. *Gifted as they are, authentic teachers do not want you to arise through them nor do they have the ability to so.* It is only through personal inner growth that you will purify and pass through "Christ consciousness", which is only a title of an evolved state of being. It has many other names by many other groupings and cultures; some that existed for ages before the newer religions. What ego to think previous cultures did not discover and reach the epitome of inner evolution.

Allow the "first coming" to be the envelopment and receiving inside your own soul of the bestowal and recognition of "universal divine love consciousness" or what name you prefer. *For you will see that reality is being and living within the context of the soul-self in a glorious world filled with the joyous adventures of sharing light.* For some this is no longer even considered spiritual or religious; it is just the way it is. Do you wish to partake or not?

The first coming that is necessary is each individual reawakening to their own god-consciousness. Stop waiting for something to happen outside yourself. There is nothing out there. Do not surrender to a myth that will not happen (a second coming) and if someone is claiming to be "the one", be careful and trust your inner messages to learn from your own soul and not theirs. Perhaps the better lesson is not the search for enlightenment; better to choose reliance upon your own soul's teachings rather than another's. Why not start *trusting yourself today* and experience a first or second coming within?

FALSE PREMISE

I had or have no choice.

"Choice" is often perceived as a by-product of luxury, financial ability, cultural training or having more than one option to choose from. Be open to the suggestion that choice is living life. Life is choices. If you truly think in alignment with the universal forces, the choices you make will create aliveness, happiness, health, fulfillment, expression, and wholeness no matter what the external conditional circumstances seem to be.

Life is to create original ideas of truth, love and compassion as innate awareness rather than to just have thoughts from the past flowing through, most of which are reactive responses anyway. The strength of taking responsibility in every situation and in each passing thought or newly created thought can be demonstrated, exercised and advanced. This is your pathway to mastering what truly is free will choice.

Each person in the world has the opportunity to choose to emit love, speak truth, share, care, be of service, have self-esteem, model leadership, and to be secure and safe. All external forces can be overcome. You can override even the originally chosen avenues you brought into this incarnation.

There are areas where on the surface it seems like a choice wasn't made or you had no choice. When you go to a deeper level, you will uncover a distinction or distinctions made which represent a previous choice, ruling your conscious actions today. When you clear limiting distinctions, you will receive a great gift of knowledge and resultant freedom. The most valuable realizations will bring you to your truth. By relaxing into yourself you will enable the soul to speak to you and teach you.

It is noble to recount one's entire history, from original emergence to now. Purification is the jewel that becomes uncovered. What was before is now known. This grants a true presence and the experience to live in the supreme reality of evolved consciousness; a present state of being. *Your actions are then driven by the purity of your evolution.* As you evolve, you are coming from a place inside that grows in beauty, love, innocence, collective love-principled vision, non-attachment and *modern wisdom.*

Choice is your greatest freedom, based on free will. You take with you your choices and you live by your choices. Whether easy or hard, lucrative or scant, risky or secure, *you are constantly formulating what is to come.* Why not mix together a graceful entrance, a grand performance and a fulfilling culmination for yourself. *With deep blessings of love you will conquer all that hinders your expansion and behold the wonders of the universe and their corresponding powers.*

FALSE PREMISE

Strengthen and rely upon your faith to take care
of matters and provide you with eternal life.

There are many myths, beware. No one can give you
what you already have. If they say they can, beware.
You are already an eternal spirit.

Faith oriented systems and structures base themselves on
a belief framework of allegiance, loyalty, obligation and
fidelity. The faith is taught to evoke a dependence on an
unknown outer image, being or idol. It does not provide
what is idealized. Occasional occurrences do, however,
meet the definition but are not created from the
emphasized system and structure. They are created
because they are created.

True and authentic allegiance, loyalty, obligation and
fidelity do not exist in what humanity and its authority
strata call "faith". What has been taught, indoctrinated
and practiced in the past does not make something
bonafide. Yes, people do have great reprieves from

misery, pain and suffering. Yes, people do perform faith-oriented prayer. The results are not due to faith, although it is said to be.

If you can move your awareness into a state of *real thinking*, this will make sense. There exist delays in substantive resolutions, actions, experiences and outcomes when one devotes and participates in faith. When the end result finally occurs or doesn't occur, people believe it is due to their previous demonstration of faith or something else. This is a false premise and was never meant to be a way of life.

Consciously aware persons, in alignment with universal law, do not use or interact with any sort of faith. They have untrained themselves from the dependency of faith living. Through a conscious boundary of focusing upon oneself in order to know thyself, and through directing one's energy into the world from this profound inner place of the soul, faith is non-existent. *What occurs in the world is a reflection of what is directed into the world from deep within the individual.* An adept projects wisdom and clarity into the world and does not seek upon faith as she or he already owns, knows and has mastered the ability to create and manifest into the world. The adept loves. The evolved one does not operate from need, hope or the lack of something.

Those of faith do function from need and hope, looking towards faith and outside sources to replenish and supply the desired result. They want to give to something else their responsibility in the matter. This behavior only serves to weaken humankind. Strengthen humankind acting from conscious awareness and non-attachment. You will then be able to live from a place of inner security and outcome that is always present, instead of from a waiting, wanting, hoping, prostrative and projecting lifestyle. Learn to ascertain all facts and internally educate yourself into the freedom of non-faith living. In this way, you will build trust in yourself and begin to surround yourself with real people that can be trusted. *You will have trust, not faith, in your fellow humans.* These relationships will be the most effective ones you have ever made as positive actions will follow. Exchange faith for friendship, faith for self-knowledge, faith for trust, and faith for soul originated behavior.

FALSE PREMISE

Defensive behavior is natural and necessary.

Not speaking of military defense, even though it is still totally reflective of current human condition, defensive behavior lacks positive distinctions of power. Defensive behavior is rooted in false distinctions of weakness, fantasy, and insanity.

The attachment to a false idea for one's security and safety will make one defensive in any conversation when tested. Strong verbal, facial and even physical responses are made in alliance to the false distinction, rather than a portrayal of friendliness and openness to synthesize information and knowledge. What stands between divine coalescence and opposing points of view is a false sense of identity with faulty thoughts of the past. These will regenerate at every opportunity and can enmesh further in an exponential manner. The identity is with the false distinction and not the relationship.

Spiritual living and being has no defensive behavior as the base of self-identity and awareness is love, truth and integrity. Your great teachers are not people. Your great teachers are your negative emotions and defensive behavior. They are triggered by your world and based in deeply internalized dialogue that, when reviewed, can be restructured into empowering ideas rather than ideas that hurt, crush and block your development. It is a humbling process to realize that you have made mistakes along the way in your thinking and in how you arrive at your thoughts.

The able, wise one does not hold an internal maze and webbed pattern to think through. Instead, a clear and simple holding of each new input is reviewed, corrected, improved, interconnected or rejected. There is a prequalification that each thought must pass through universally aligned principles before being accepted in. The same is true for what goes out. Courses in NLP (neuro-linguistic programming) specialize in empowerment speaking.

One of the most major flaws in human consciousness is "the failure to analyze and filter all interpretations, thoughts and impressions" before merging and storing them. Isn't it better to improve one's internal skills of processing outer and inner communications than to waste years and lifetimes on erroneous filings and defensive behavior?

FALSE PREMISE

Doomsday, Armageddon and Earth changes are
real and should be feared.

I have addressed these in the past and they are being
addressed again because they are predominant beliefs
that continue to be preached by many institutions,
organizations and individuals. Do not be led by those
who do not know and who only wish to instill fear and
impose authority. Their false premises are not worthy to
be foundational distinctions driving your life's decisions.
It is not for you to make decisions and take actions based
upon erroneous ideas and fear. It is for you to discern
what is fact and take actions based upon truth and love.
You will create a stable foundation and outcome for
yourself and family when you operate from internal soul
alignment, not the storytelling of "the end is near" by
certain religions and "the earth will incur a pole shift
which will only leave the good people unharmed" by

certain new age groups. *Fantasy only brings more layerings of fantasy.*

Here are some facts about the earth's rhythmic balanced interchange that the new age has yet to learn. The north to south magnetic pole is positioned by the rotation of the planet. The rotation and position of the planet is determined by its magnetic standing in the galaxy. The planets of our solar system are being drawn slowly towards our sun. The sun and moon influence and determine weather patterns. Ozone holes influence weather and the seas; they will not shift the poles. Occasional earthquakes, volcanic eruptions, floods, etc., are natural to the earth. Humanity's recorded history is a minuscule amount of time in eternity. The interpretations that have been made from these lean recordings is unfounded. Even as I look back through all time at the planet, there exists no pattern or consistency for interpreted human meaning and assumptions. What occurs just occurs and it is random. Can you not accept that life is just as it is? Can you stop putting such importance upon the ideology of the human species which is often false? Please bring love and peace and service to the world. You can live inside your compassion for one another instead of portrayals and inheritances of fear and fantasy.

FALSE PREMISE

People think information is power. People think that technology is power.

In this technological age, people have said that information is power, even more powerful than money. In 1964, Marshall McLuhan wrote in a letter to Buckminster Fuller, "If one says that any new technology creates a new environment, that is better than saying the medium is the message. The content of the new environment is always the old one. The content is greatly transformed by the new technology." For some, the medium is the power. I say that the real power or the best and strongest power, setting aside the conversation of whether there is or is not such a thing as power, is

1987 Letters of Marshall McLuhan, Oxford University Press p.308-309 Marshall McLuhan (1911-1980) author, lecturer, teacher who was prominent in the 1960s and 1970s. Buckminster Fuller (1895-1983), American architect and engineer noted for his revolutionary technological designs based on the Dymaxion principle - that of gaining maximum results from minimum material and energy. McLuhan had met Fuller at the 1962 Delos symposium.

something else. *Finely tuned discernment resulting in clear distinctions is power. The distinction excellence creates advanced contexts of perception and vision.* The medium or information may change through the ages; the distinctions develop further in your discerning and constant search of excellence. May you move beyond the false premises of information or mediums and to the enhancing of your ability and capacity to discern reality and distinctly define its laws. You will live in the state of love and bliss derived from your mastery of distinction. Then you will make the ultimate distinction - love is all there is. Does that make love the ultimate power or the result of true power? Both, when you make the distinction! Enjoy!

Unlearning the general thought conditioning that these and other false premises pervade will release you into a new space to exercise discernment and inner direction like never before. Take these into serious consideration before pursuing the five basic Oracle Teachings, and you will excel in your self-development with independence. It is time to learn to know thyself and live by the natural energy flow of our benevolent universe. *Lift yourself out of the deep indoctrination of the outer world and be guided by the purity of your heart and soul. The fundamental truths will be your stepping stones to authentic authority and vision.*

You are the cause in the matter of every experience, interaction and thought. Responsible living involves two sides in participation, whether it is a dance of love or darkness. You can dance with the light, or without it.

All experience is a current or an after-the-fact reflection of your inner foundation. If you live and breathe purity, you will be engulfed in the bounty of all that the universe can direct onto your stage of life. If you live and breathe from a faulty foundation of many or remaining erroneous distinctions you will reap what you have sown. If you are a strong public speaker, you will speak. If you are timid, you will not. There are past experiences and absorbed misconceptions, sanctimonious wisdom, inner issues and false premises that keep you from your wholeness.

You create all experiences, good and not good. Some are created from good or false distinctions made 1,500 years ago, 20,000 years ago, 100 years ago, etc. It is for you to rediscover where you made the turn from the light. You cannot find this turn through another, it takes place from your voluntary search within for self-discovery. Expose yourself to yourself and you will see your holiness and thrive in the celebration of unity and grace. You will control the feedback of the universe to portray the life you knew you could have and were not aware of how to obtain.

Regain your power and retrieve yourself. Take back your life and live from an inner direction of mastery, not an enslaved subordination to external circumstances and treatment. The knowledge you gain will be a homecoming to the brilliance of your soul. You do know the way. It is your way. By listening to your soul's soft voice, you will return and be simply . . . free.

Become the presence of noble sacred oneness.

ORACLE

CHAPTER THREE

THE ORACLE TEACHINGS

The Oracle Teachings were originally developed for my own personal processing to reveal my true soul-self once again to myself and, later, to the world. Each has been tested thoroughly to give the expected results that I demand for great leaps in transformation. I do not believe in spending a lot of time for change and purification. It is unnecessary to strain, dwell upon or lengthen the time going through the tunnel of transformation. Walk into the lake of divinity and leave the safety of the shoreline by enveloping yourself in the light and by giving the light your listening. It may be a humbling experience for some of you to stop and listen. You will hear the pure guidance that you need to access in order to evolve quickly. Let go of all complicated or restrictive behaviors or practices. Instead, learn of the Oracle Teachings and see them in practice in the following chapters. Your soul will be eternally grateful to be freed from the grip of the mind and its limitations.

The five basic, profound Oracle Teachings are to be used in any sequence and at anytime. They are simple so that you can enter into their use on your own. You see, they are not tools, steps, or practices of any sort. *They are the basic forms of communication between the physical and metaphysical bodies and the universe. That is all. It was never meant to be a struggle or a mystery, the universe is simple and simplified.* So much so, that humanity does not see it, hear it or feel it. You can custom design your time in the tunnel of transformation. Just be aware that if you are not moving along well enough, perhaps it is best to ask for deep receivings of divine love to be able to use your inner messages to their maximum benefit.

There are five primary Oracle Teachings. So know that they have withstood the tests of time. I have experienced these through the ages. They are presented for your benefit in contemporary language. My soul sings as I am reminded of the first time I received the bestowal of divine light in my first meditation when I was 27 years old. To reconnect at a conscious level is one of the greatest gifts to receive for oneself and to give to another. Know that you will always be blessed with golden, sacred and holy light.

Oracle Teaching Number One

The Divine Love Meditation

We have been raised to show affection to family and close friends. There is more. We have been taught to worship and adore. There is more. You can replace worship and adoration with constructive inner communication achieved in meditation communion. You can see and feel the unconditional love of all that is, in interactive meditation. This sincere blessing from the universe is always present just waiting to be received into your soul through interactive meditation. The first basic, profound Oracle Teaching is the interactive meditation of divine love. You will be graced and blessed in pure love that is stronger than anything you have experienced in life. The exchange of receiving the light and giving yourself to the receiving may have been forgotten. It is now and always has been available to you. You may begin to renew yourself in the power of the golden holy light of the pure and sacred energy of our existence.

The divine love meditation gives you the power to interact with the universe's wisdom, truth, guidance and love. You will see and feel the natural state of ecstasy. This is all possible for humanity. To live in the glory of love and to radiate its wonders of peace, kindness, knowledge and vision.

To enter into the divine love meditation, it is best to relax the body, close your eyes and ask your mind to surrender to your soul's guidance. A serene environment, with soft music, the flow of a stream or ocean waves, or just plain silence, all set the proper stage to be able to hear your soul speak. The soul speaks through your inner ear's hearing. It comes through telepathic exchanges with the pure divine love of the universe and your authentic soul-self.

Once relaxed, look with your inner sight at your heart center. Ask your own inner, golden light of love from your soul, based at the heart, to unveil itself and expand throughout your body, the room, into the earth and into the sky and the ether. Expand your soul and release it from the repression of your chest. As you do so, there will be a sense of relief, a sense of centeredness and a sense of freedom. You may be in awe to see your inner soul light expand to its natural large size.

At this point, you may start to ask for the golden light of the pure divine love to begin to grace your soul with the inflow of its love. Look above your head and see a bright shining, golden star of light, one to two yards/meters above. Ask the divine love light to flow into your crown from this star center. The golden light will then fulfill your sincere request and feed your soul reservoir and refill it. You will see the soft waves of the unconditional, eternal love flowing into your energy (aura, spirit, light, soul) body and your physical body. You will see your aura expanding. You will feel that you are being loved and bathed by the holy light. Receive as much as you want. Ask the divine love to increase its potency and the inflow will become stronger. With it comes the peacefulness you have been searching for.

There are no secrets to oneness, only the doorway of asking to receive its grace and allowing yourself the time to be still and to be blessed with its light. Simple as it may sound, this is the way it is. No exercises, no contortions, no mantras, no devotion, no worship, no adoration, no hierarchy, no offerings, no gender limitations, no age limitations, no race limitations, no income limitations are asked of you by the universe and its love. It is only for you to ask for the receiving of the divine love in meditation.

Continue to ask for deeper and more concentrated bestowals of the inflow of golden universal divine love light to flow into your crown, heart and soul, and body. See the waves of light become thicker and brighter with each inflow. Feel the love more and more as you become more aware of its divine presence. *This is our holy spiritual energy being one with the sacred energy of reality.* When your soul reservoir feels full, you can slowly end the embrace of divine love to integrate and balance the newly expanded field of your soul and energy body. You will feel a sense of having been embraced in this love and knowing that you are safe in the pureness of it.

After a while, you will be able to receive inflows of light during any normal daytime activities, as you can activate the receiving with only your sincere thought to access it once again. You can bless others with this sacred light, also. Know that we are all nurtured by the divine love and are best guided by its love and messages of wisdom; messages that will propel you into the heights of purity.

Oracle Teaching number one is to directly receive the divine love by asking for it to infuse your precious soul. The two basic words are ask and receive. This is so basic that humankind overlooks this profoundly simple gateway. *Your willingness to return to the simplicity in order to achieve enlightenment is a masterful move.*

Please read the next teaching to learn how to access messages from the universal light.

Oracle   Teaching   Number   Two

Interactive   Communion   for   Guidance

Once you feel your soul reservoir has been replenished with universal divine love, ask for your soul to integrate further and breathe away the mental controls that have been holding on. Ask your mind to continue to surrender to your soul. Use your inner sight to walk into a sacred sanctuary setting of your choice. A sanctuary is a self-chosen environment that contains the natural elements, landscape and beauty you love. It is here that you will sit or lay down your soul-self to receive your spiritual guidance by listening to the holy light, your guides or the truth within you.

Interactive communion for guidance is both inner and outer communication with your spirit guides, angels, guardians, helpers, and others you have known or do not know. As you relax in your sanctuary you will reach a point where you feel very nurtured and comforted by the divine love light. You will know that you are ready to receive your learnings and teachings. This is the point in your meditation where you softly and sincerely ask for your guide(s) to gently and lovingly enter your sanctuary. You will see them appear through the faculty of inner sight and they will walk up to you. They will emit light and the vibration of love to your entire being. Ask them to sit by you. See the sacred energy of their spirit or spirits.

In this place of pure vibration, your helper or helpers appear and begin to exchange knowledge and guidance telepathically with you. Listen to their wise words, sent into your inner hearing without movement of their lips. It is here that you will hear. You can ask questions and express your concerns. The soft, yet profound, inner voice of your soul will speak the messages back to you in the center of your head where your inner ear is located. You will know that its source is truth and not your mind, as the wording is advanced and elevated. It is telepathically transferred to your inner hearing and inner sight. The exchange is very fast and complete. This teaching adds velocity to propel yourself into purification. Listen, learn and lift your consciousness into the unity of divinity consciousness. Just the hearing of the guidance will not purify all of your issues at once, however, it is caring direction and wise guidance. They know what you need.

It is up to you to freely direct yourself into purity from your own sheer will and desire to do so. Your commitment to transform and your dedication to make self-discovery a priority in your life will be very rewarding.

It does not matter whether you believe in guides or angels, the results will speak for themselves. The important point is to elevate your level of consciousness with truth, knowledge and love. Through inner communion (meditation) you will be able to achieve the supreme awareness that will fulfill your destiny and leave your soul filled with divine love for yourself and for you to give to the world.

Oracle Teaching number two is to receive the wise messages that guidance will provide. The key words are listen and hear. You will know they are the words that create the keystones to your evolution. Be still and allow yourself to interactively commune with your special guides and guardians who love and watch over you.

Oracle Teaching Number Three

Soul Remembrance for Purification

The third Oracle Teaching is a visual cleansing of the energy spirit body many call the aura, etheric or causal. I call it the soul, pure and simple, that has been *impressioned* with false distinctions of the mind. The impressions, when cleared, quickly evolve and purify the being, as the soul returns to its natural state.

As you deepen your presence or concentration in your sanctuary in divine love meditation, you reach a place where you feel the processing of your past can begin on a deeper, more intense level. In this advanced and relaxed state, you can start viewing with your inner sight, the eternal energy, the spirit body, the soul. If you take a look at yourself from a distance with your inner sight, you can clearly view your soul's light body. Begin to scan the energy body thoroughly from this place. Or, if you prefer, use your inner sight to view your soul minutely by scanning side to side, right to left and left to right, from inside your physical body and the soul body.

In the pure golden light of your soul-self, there will occasionally appear to be darker spheres of energy holdings. They can appear to be as small as a pebble and as large as a football ball or larger. As you scan thoroughly, you will see one appear at an appropriate place. Surround it with the divine love and its golden light and ask it to unfold to its full natural size. This field of energy has been held in your soul's spirit body for a short period of time or through the ages, waiting to be acknowledged and heard. It is through the remembrance of your soul's history that the real blocks and true limitations of your past become revealed. As you track the energy in the gray (or other color) field, let it lead you to its source - the time, location, circumstances and dynamics under which it was created. You view the events as if watching a video screen. The message is clear and directs you to different experiences in a past incarnation that begin to piece together your reactive self and what the facts were at the time. The gray energy field will unfold the scenes and conversations of your past existence. It is like a time message capsule going off with an important playback of an experience in your past. You will see and feel your inner self during the re-experience. It is in this review that you will rediscover what false distinction was made up by your mind to rule your future actions and behavior. By realizing what the distinction was, you can let it go and move into the knowledge of what really occurred and release the limiting mental thought. This freedom expands the soul, places love into the space where this gray energy was holding, and brings wellness to the body. It does not matter whether you believe in past lives or not, the conscious state of a person excels, regardless. Some prefer to believe it is dream symbology or imagination, and interpret the symbols for useful transformation.

Some people prefer to feel their way back into their soul remembrance rather than cleanse the soul visually. This is another way to purify for evolution, and it is just as effective. Connect with a negative emotion or thought that is fairly strong to sense and which repeats itself in your life. The emotion will lead you back to a time in your past when you had an uncomfortable experience. It will lead you to the exact experiences that caused the emotion to take seed in your soul's energy body.

Still another way that you can recognize and release the past is to ask a question or seek to release blocks to prosperity, happiness, relationship, etc. You will be guided back into your soul history by your soul's willingness to release the limiting distinction or distinctions.

All three of these entrances to the self work well and the results are relief, release, and rejuvenation of the soul-self. The remembrance teaching gives you the inner strength to unravel the mind's twisted controls, see how they were created and the confidence to discard them for truth, wisdom, knowledge, self-trust, self-expression and love. The cleansing of your spirit brings clarity and the power of being an unveiled soul operating as soul over mind.

The greatest stories ever told are the ones you have been secretly carrying inside all these years. *Relax and retrieve your past to create your present self. Know that it is only a matter of a "complete review" between you and a life of enlightened living.*

Oracle Teaching number three is to replay and research your past to gain the state of present awareness. The prime words are remember and relate. *You will enter your prime through the perfection of your soul remembrances. The power of soul over mind will be discovered and conquered as you use the teachings and re-integrate the soul.*

Oracle Teaching Number Four

The Sacred Place Meditation

Throughout the ages the adept ones have found the deep sacred place within. I am speaking of the very deep place within that is so deep it is called the sacred place. It is a sacred place that has been searched for by millions of people in the past. Only a few have found it. Only a few know how to or desire to share with others the way to it.

Once you reconnect with the sacred place do not let it go. It is a profound place. It is a powerful place. It is a simple place. *It is a place where one feels the vast freedom of all consciousness.* In this place you clearly see the formula for creating and manifesting from nothing; from silence into words, thoughts, energy and form. *Each desire contains within itself the capacity to emerge out into the universe with a force that creates completion, fulfillment, commitment and promise.* The fourth teaching is a major passage into the knowledge of how the universe truly works. Be at peace in the still space and co-create with it.

Many traditional religions and spiritual systems have used the inner sight of the third (or single) eye at the center of the eyebrows and forehead. People are taught to concentrate here for creative visualization, remote viewing, and intuitive messages. This place of visualization is not the place of power; it is only the viewing screen. The power center is in what I call the fourth eye, located at the back of the head at the occipital bone. This is the place where you perhaps have felt that you have had eyes out the back of your head. It is easy to enter the fourth eye. In fact, all of the Oracle Teachings are simple and easily accessed!

Why is this place not well known? Has it been hidden from us by the religious hierarchies? Do they know of it or are they unaware of it? Let me explain the path to the fourth eye and the sacred place it beholds. After you have reached a state of fullness from the inflow of the divine love meditation, take the next step of bringing your awareness to the back of your head. Begin visualizing the golden light becoming brighter and brighter there. Allow it to grow and glow. After a few minutes, ask the divine light to lead you deeper into the fourth eye as if you are entering a black hole in the universe. Follow the divine energy back, back, further and further out. Continue following it deeper and deeper into the darkness until you enter the place where you can see the shining stars of the universe surround you. Relax in this sacred place and behold the deep stillness and silence. This is the *fulcrum* space where you can truly rest, relieve stress, and release all connections to preconceived ideas and conditioning. It is so worthwhile to stay in this place of silence and to feel the profoundness of what exists before all words, before all thoughts and before all desires!

After you feel filled with the sacred peace of this meditation, take the next step. Begin using the clearing to create. Watch and see your authentic thoughts, words and visions being created before your inner sight by viewing from the sacred place of the fourth eye through to the third eye. It is like watching the wind form clouds in front of you from miles away. It is like projecting a movie from the fourth eye onto the third eye screen. In the past, people have become enamored with the movie rather than focusing their power on the projector at the fourth eye. *It is from here that your power to manifest is formulated.* You will carry your idea from energy into powerful existence which will then begin manifesting immediately in the world.

Oracle Teaching number four is the sacred meditation that exists in the true place for thinking. It is the place where true creativity is brought to life. The two words of empowerment of teaching number four are *clarity and creativity.* May you honor yourself with this powerful centering place and be fully graced and blessed with its teachings.

Oracle   Teaching   Number   Five

Interactive   Progression   Meditation

The first four teachings fill you with light, cleanse the past, evolve you into sacred knowledge and into the still place of grand creativity, manifestation and peace. The fifth teaching is used to see where you are headed in your life. In other words, you can look into your future to see where you are going, from your current state of consciousness. Using *interactive progression meditation*, you can see if you will be creating and achieving your goals. The visions and inner messages can act as guidelines and feedback. You will know if you have developed your evolution to the state that fulfills you and supplies your needs. It is an interactive meditation that gives confirmation. Not all is always revealed, only what can be presented for your level of understanding. Sometimes it is best to leave the unfoldment to its natural time and to not try to see it all before it happens. *I do not advise an overuse of interactive progression meditation.*

The power is in purifying, and all progression will be gifts of natural alignment with universal law and unity.

After you are in a relaxed and filled soul reservoir state, as described in Teaching One, you can enter into the interactive progression meditation, Teaching Five. It is here that you will see the beginnings of what you are sowing now. This is primarily to be used as a guideline to help and confirm that you are on track with your goals.

In this place of peace, ask your soul to show you where you will be in two or three years. Your inner sight will give you a vision which is full of information. Be careful to interpret what you see properly, so as to not misdirect yourself in life. You may also ask questions regarding other matters to give you feedback on health, relationships, goal achievement, warnings, outcomes of projects, appraisal of others, and more. You will receive visual responses or telepathic worded messages or both. Use what you want and know that, as you increase your communications with your soul and the divine universe, you will develop your metaphysical skills. So much so, that it becomes easier and faster to know thyself and become purer and purer.

Oracle Teaching number five is about checking into your progress. The important words are *guidelines and feedback. The interactive progression meditation will import to your present outlook the primary mirroring of your current projection of inner creation.* It is here that you learn what is missing or what may be too strong in your approach to reach your goals. If you draw a blank during the meditation, it usually just means the inquiry is not worthy of a reply, that it is premature for you to see yet, or that you are temporarily distracted. *Build your self-trust, and the universe will surround you with her generous gifts and many embraces of endearment.*

I now share with humanity the five main Oracle Teachings which I have developed, and used. They are profound both singly and united, creating the gateway and empowerment structure to unveil the soul and release the restrictive mind. They are all natural communication paths to yourself, your guides and the universe. They are not processes, methods, steps, rituals or tools. They are proven, direct communications of true communion with our divine universe, telepathy with your guardians and resonance with your soul-self.

The following chapters will give you insight into and confirmation of the unique and honoring direction that has assisted those who have used the Oracle Teachings. They too are and were on the path of *self-re-discovery*. With permission, I am able to share their individual historical remembrances so that you, too, can see the results which the teachings produce. *Through the self-reliant being, all may be seen, heard and felt. Go forth and step blissfully into your past, with willing heart and begin to open to your soul and be free.*

CHAPTER FOUR

SHARINGS OF THE ORACLE TEACHINGS

Through their commitment to self-reliant evolution, the following individuals have unveiled their souls to provide a circle of sharing for the enhancement of your journey. For some it was an easy journey and for some it was emotional and difficult, each learning in their own way to see the soul-self and erase the limiting grip of the mind. May you learn from their experiences and gain the inner strength to use the teachings for your own evolution. For convenience, the following soul history remembrances are in order by youngest age first. The women have had male incarnations and the men have had female incarnations. Even though there are more women sharing their experiences, the teachings work beyond gender, age, race, and background. Know that you too can make tremendous advances in your evolution as these people have. Take what you want from their experiences and walk into your remembrances to unveil

the grace and power of your own soul.

Soul Remembrance

Female, Age 13

Many wise parents teach their young to meditate with the divine love and support their purification of the past. After weeks of absence from school, this young goddess was feeling unwell from liver complications, eczema rashes, and indigestion. Whenever an upset occurred at school, she would retreat home and withdraw from school. This pattern of behavior began to worry her parents. Gentle and caring as they were, the natural remedies being used lasted only for short periods of time and a relapse would happen. Not wanting to take too much more time to resolve the behavior pattern creating the physical symptoms, the mother, who was newly introduced to the Oracle Teachings, asked that her daughter be given the opportunity to learn them as well.

With soft music in the background and lying comfortably on a large futon, I guided the young goddess to see the golden divine love light of the universe and receive the bestowal of the holy energy: Oracle Teaching number one. She was very open to receiving the sacred essence and was able to additionally see her guardian angels surrounding her, Oracle Teaching number two. For her, the inner sight and hearing faculties were intact. In fact, for most children they are still functioning very strongly.

After filling her soul reservoir with divine love, she then was guided to begin using the inner scanning process, Oracle Teaching number three, to locate the largest gray energy mass that was hovering in her energy body. It was very large and hovered around her liver. We guided it to rise above the physical body and radiate its energy stronger so that she could really take hold of its frequency and follow it back in her divine remembrance to the place and time when it began as cause. It turned out that several causes were fueling it from several different incarnations. We had time to review only two of the causes, which reduced the size of the gray energy field dramatically. One cause was a life during the 1700-1800s when she was a young boy. The young boy's close friend had died and he did not know how to process his mourning and loss. He never did. The grieving was buried deep inside. It was being carried in thought in the gray energy field in her spirit body. After seeing this she realized she could let go of the sorrow and replace it with love. She did so. She then sent her young boy friend from that past a strong wave of her undying love. It was resolved.

The other incarnation experience was as a young girl in the 1800s being scolded for something she did not say or do. She was not able to be heard that it was not she who did it and was punished for it anyway. This accounts for her withdrawal from unfounded sternness and reprimanding in this life; therefore, the reclusive behavior at home. Having seen this, she was able to understand her sensitivity to harsh treatment and knew she could stand up for herself better in the present and future.

This young goddess was able to go into her soul history knowing that her guardian angels were by her side and it was a safe process. She then received further inflows and nurturing of the golden divine love light. Afterwards, she had a radiant glow about her and said she felt better and could feel the waves of unconditional love flow into her soul. She can now work further on her purification with her mother. Her physical body will respond to the clearings. She is an advanced soul to have asked for the divine love at such a young age.

When you truly open yourself to the idea that there are possibilities available for clearing the way to enlightenment through the power of divine love, soul remembrance, interactive communion, sacred place knowledge and progression, the purification will begin. This young goddess was able to heal considerably in only one hour. In fact, within two months, her blood test showed the liver had recovered completely and she was consistently attending classes. What will you bring to yourself using the Oracle Teachings? As simple they may be, the results are major.

As I look into her soul and mind matrix I see that she will flourish as a young woman. Her will to shine from her heart and its purity will radiate with her innocence. She will learn to grow in her development of close friendship, as she is no longer mourning a loss inside. She can create friendship without the outcome of sadness. She is a very pretty and sweet young goddess.

Soul   Remembrance

Male, Age 36

This experience will surprise you. In less than three hours, he received the complete mystical enlightenment experience. To understand the intensity of this, he is an intellectual who never made time to meditate. He had channeled and experienced visual meditations occasionally, when with others. He is quite active in external activities and relationships and did not yet have the inner understanding that the universal divine light is his foundation and make-up. He was a skeptic of the Oracle Teachings. His controlling mind was severely dominating his soul. The first hour involved enveloping him in the pure golden light of the universe. He was not familiar with the energy and was hesitant to begin. I suggested that he could come back the next evening as this would allow his mind to feel more comfortable with the light and to prepare for surrendering to his soul.

He laid down on the private session table and was asked to relax. Overnight his mind seemed to develop enough curiosity to allow us to continue. When I viewed his spirit body, there loomed three large gray energy fields which were based in fear. His mind held these very strongly and they were blocking his soul light. The three fears were: fear of poverty, fear of insanity and fear of spiritual awareness. He clings to his inherited fortune in this life, clings to his intellectualism and academia in this life and buffers himself from spirituality as he has seen many spiritually gifted people martyred in past lifetimes. With the grace and bestowal of the divine love meditation, these fears were removed by the third hour. Through the receiving, renewing and refilling with the divine love, he surrendered to his soul. This enabled him to let go and not have to hold everything together to protect himself.

He learned how to skillfully bring the light into his soul in a way that widens and clears the corridors between the power vortices of the body. It is very easy to achieve when using the golden light. As we were enhancing the thymus center, it happened. Something gave way in the corridor and the blockage was dramatically swept away. In one big inflow he was engulfed fully by the golden divine love light! The divine love powerfully filled the entire room as well! He resonated in this mystical energy for a long time. For the rest of the evening he was amazed and dazed at seeing "true reality" for the first time.

When we were clearing his corridor, we were working from the feet upwards. Usually I would work from the crown downwards on the body. It was when the thymus was reached that the enlightenment took place. Many practices advise you that the throat and heart area are centers to be worked on. They seem either to not know or to ignore the power of the thymus area. It is one of the most common energy blocked areas in the human body.

In a short time, he met his soulmate and moved to a new home, still curious and cautious, yet transformed by seeing "true reality".

The enlightenment experience will clear away many of your former ideas and context of how you view yourself and the world. As you continue to use the divine love you will be blessed with more knowledge and the empowerment always leads you back to soul over mind. Let go of your mental restrictions for the advances of your soul. This sharing shows that even a novice meditator can receive the great divine experience.

Soul   Remembrance

Female, Age 40

People carry and repeat their patterns until they are cleared. This one was very anxious to receive the Oracle Teachings and transcend her past. Her faculties were already developed, just untapped. She had two separate appointments several months apart for a total approximate time of 1.5 hours and one meditation of her own for an hour while on holiday. See what she transcended using the divine love in only 2.5 hours of accumulative time . . .

In her first meditation, she received enlightening brilliant and bold golden shafts of pure light flowing into her crown and spirit body. It was very strong, clear and an amazing feeling of being refilled with spiritual love. Once renewed in the state of oneness, she forged ahead. As she began to scan her field of light she came upon a dark sphere located at her throat. She started to track its signal backward in her soul's remembrance to the exact time, place and experience when it was conceived.

She was 30 years old in the medieval period. There were power and control games. If you spoke out the result would be death. The false distinction she created from that culture was, "Don't speak-up because you get murdered." Upon this review, she released the suppressing gray sphere from her throat and replaced the void with golden divine love light. In her current life she has not spoken out and prefers to listen to everyone else in the room. She is a good listener and does contribute, however, primarily on a one on one basis. See how the next soul remembrance ties in.

She went to the next gray energy sphere in her body. It was located in her stomach. She tracked its frequency back to when it began. It was the 1800s in America. She was a child of eight to 10 years of age. She did not like the food or the living situation she was in. Her family decided to move and she saw herself on a carriage moving to another place, strange and new, against her will. She was subjected to her parents' choices and had to go along. She could not have what she really wanted as a dependent child without power. A few years later she began to paint. Through her artwork she found freedom. She found that she could trade her art for the things she wanted. This did not last. Her parents did not want to allow her to trade. She was shut down again. Her needs were not being met and her creativity was suppressed. She made up three false distinctions: "I am controlled. My independence is taken away. You must 'survive' in the environment." With an amazing feeling of spiraling light energy flowing inside and being freed up inside her a new positive distinction was birthed in place: "Be creative!"

She is now moving into a new awareness of herself to speak her truth and express her creativity without any fear, control or restrictions. In her second meditation she scanned her throat area again and it was clear. Her messages within and with her spirit guides were of feeling safe and not threatened. She felt and saw her women ancestors who were supportive as guides. They were strong and told her it was okay to be strong and just get used to feeling strong. She felt really supported by them and could call on them at anytime. This gave her an additional sense of security!

When on holiday, with her family and relatives

by a large lake, she found herself outside alone by a fire. Everyone had gone inside the cabin as it became dark. She was with the stars, sky, water, the entire environment and stillness. She felt centered outside. She quietly went into meditation.

Normally she would go along and take care of everyone's needs and be with them. On this night she heard herself inside say, "It is okay not to participate and be comfortable for myself." She saw the distinction of choice. She could choose to go in and be with the relatives or just sit outside and not mix when she didn't want to. The choice and the strength to make the choice were hers. She didn't have to go back in to be with them or to be with people. It didn't and doesn't matter. The power is in her strength to meet her needs of space. The family members may make up stories about her choices and they will just be their stories, not hers. It is healthier for her to be true to herself and ultimately healthier for them. As you change the dynamics of relating the others are forced to shift as well or remove themselves from the relationship.

Her time alone by the lake gave her sacred moments with

her soul, her guides and the cosmos. She can live her life not driven by what should be done, rather by what is in her alignment to do. In her experience of divine love meditation she regains her truth and sees her real soul-self. The fulfillment of the divine love inflow to fill the soul's reservoir empowers her self-trust to take the next steps forward in self-expression. Her actions will not be driven for family approval, they will arise from self approval. She has purchased new beautiful clothing, was taken on a foreign holiday, expanded her beach house, is spending more time in her garden, which she loves, and is reducing the amount of days she works each week counseling. She is taking actions that fulfill her needs. Her family will benefit from her modeling and her own satisfaction.

By affirming your own being you allow yourself to be. May your inner beauty and gifts flourish in your sea of self-love.

Soul   Remembrance

Male,   Age   45

A breakthrough life is unfolding for this special one after retrieving and overcoming seven major false distinctions he had been recycling through the ages. They were deep blocks relating to fear, endurance, prosperity, personal relationship and one's place in the universe.

Obviously, recounting the details cannot bring the same power and aliveness as his remembrance experiences. Just know that they were extremely powerful and transformed his life within minutes, hours and days. So much so, that he accomplished the following: He transformed from earning $500 per week to $500 per hour. He met, married and is now living with his soulmate. He lost 20 pounds, started playing golf and boogie boarding, improved his health and vitality. He lives in happiness instead of the mental hindrances of his past. He has answered his deepest spiritual questions. This is an extraordinary individual who chose to take his evolution into his own hands - or shall we say, into his own soul!

To walk in fear instead of love is a scary way to live. He had often wondered where it came from when it would surface inside. One day it finally revealed itself in meditation. He had been walking in fear and self-protection and did not understand why it would reappear and bring such discomfort inside his chest. He began to track the fear by allowing it to become very strong and asked it to lead him back to the experience where it began. The soul remembrance brought him clearly to the cause. It is an experience that many have shared and carry in their souls.

This gentle man remembered being brought against his will into an area where lions were held. He could feel the trembling in the cells of his body, particularly his chest. There was so much pure fear. He did not have any defensive weapons or tools with which to protect himself. Then he knew, it was this fear of approximately 2000 years ago that he had been carrying inside. The trembling fear reached a fever pitch as the lion leapt straight at him and began to rip his chest apart. He died in fear, pain, helplessness and victimization.

After the soul remembrance of this incident, he released a major holding in his body and psyche and has had skyrocketing results in life, no longer operating defensively or protectively from fear. He now *projects his worthiness* to the world instead. By letting go of the past he can now live in the present without fear.

Another past experience was revealed in meditation. It was in the south of the U.S. He was a black male slave whose family had grown up in slavery. He personally never had any children of his own. He didn't sense that he was poorly treated, however. He recalled being set free around the age of 50 and worked his way up North. He ended up working on the railroads around St. Louis. It was a long hard life and yet he seemed to maintain some sense of self respect. He had to go through endurance and a somewhat lonely life. He died as a free man in his mid 60s.

This soul remembrance freed up the sense of being a slave to other people's whims and requests. Even household chores would bother him at times. The regression allowed him to gain more self-esteem and realize even in this modern world people have to do menial tasks and that doesn't make them "lowly" or "less than" other people. It is okay to do them just because they need to be done.

Still, he had another slave life. It was in Egypt. Briefly, he saw himself as part of a grueling slave work crew moving big stones for various construction projects. There was no complaining to be done. It was at such a survival level of "work or die". He learned stamina, yet it was fueled from a basis to survive. There was a broken surrendering of his spirit that "this is the way it is"; you couldn't change it. He was nothing other than a slave. After the regression, he realized he had spent many years in his current life in "endurance" circumstances and could now see a way to clear the remaining ones and be truly free. He doesn't have to put up with certain situations. He can change them and make life better for himself.

There is more. In early England, this man was a rural financial manager of serf workers in the agricultural fields. He was wealthy and he was unclear about money. Greed based, he exploited the workers. When he recalled this behavior, the antique Queen Anne styled desk he would work from appeared in view and brought forth many memories. As he explored that life to learn how he came to his current relationship with money in this life, a great false distinction spoke within and exposed itself: "Money is associated with evil doings." After all, he had earned his money by exploiting the efforts of others. As well, he did it in a way that robbed people of their dignity and self-esteem. Hence, he was blocking himself from successful prosperity in this lifetime. Once the erroneous distinction was abandoned, by seeing the falsehood of it, an immediate realignment for success and receiving of money was consciously created. Within a few days, he signed several large contracts and generated an income never before seen by him.

Classes, courses and counseling may have their place in society; now many are preferring purification for empowerment and enlightenment. Through releasing impure ideas that restrain your natural expression and beingness, you purify and evolve.

Let's move on to another remembrance of his. During the 1800s in Europe, he was a female who had a "romance" block. She was a countess of 30 years of age who fell in love with the 25 year old stable boy. Her father would not allow the relationship for class differences, so she opted for a life of money, power and stability.

Eventually, the stable boy married another. Her father died and she inherited everything. Suitors would call on her and she felt lonely. None seemed to create magic in her. Then, at the age of 45, she found love again. A 43 year old handsome, warm, friendly, funny, loving and romantic man joined her and they lived out their lives, happy and in love.

There was some residue from that life into his current one. He always had time periods of holding back from romance. He was great when he could express it. However, he was inconsistent in romantic expression within his relationship. Many people are. Once this remembrance was made, it created a complete clearing and he now is consistently romantic in his personal relationship. He gave up the separation of the false distinction of "money or love", and chose to have it all. He does have it all now.

Another self-created driving false distinction occurred in

a more recent incarnation. The misconception fueled a lifestyle of doing everything to make sure he would be loved. If he wasn't a good boy or a nice guy, he thought he wouldn't be loved. In fact, his foundation was that he would not be loved, that he would be aborted and killed. He chose his mother this lifetime to be safe. She was someone who just wanted a good boy. He did this to survive and not be killed again.

To be loved, he would subjugate himself and not express his own needs in being loved. He did not meet his needs because of a great need of approval from others for safety. In his relationships with women, he would shut down to be loved and suppress his own inner needs. Of course the relationships would eventually wither and end. He could not yet create being himself *and* being in a relationship. There was too much fear blocking. The block came from a soul remembrance of seeing himself as a fetus being miscarried by the natural mother. The false distinction he drew when disconnecting his soul from the fetus was that "he wasn't loved" and was aborted. Each future incarnation he would repeat this fear-based pattern in relationship. He therefore blocked successful relating and exchange of true deep love. After the review he felt a tremendous burden lift from his chest and has enjoyed the bliss of romance and marriage. He is now no longer willing to sacrifice his own needs for his partner's or others' needs.

One of the most important points of soul remembrance evolution is that you and only you are responsible for creating the false distinctions, misconceptions and erroneous ideas that limit your expression, aliveness and fulfillment. No one else creates your thoughts and your choices. All that you need and do is based on your thoughts and your willingness to take responsibility.

There is more. The following experience actually took place before the previous remembrances described above. When this man gave up his resistance of the divine love and allowed himself a divine love meditation, he had the second profound unity experience of his life! He finally asked in his meditation for the divine love to flow in, to fill him ---- and it did! At that moment, a riddle that had been puzzling him since his first unity consciousness experience of seven years before was answered. Who was it that had spoken into his left ear seven years prior and said, "I am the power. I am the unity."? The answer that immediately brought him into merry tears, just as the original statement did, was: "I did." At that moment, he was one with all. All was one in divine love consciousness. He laughed and cried for a couple of hours, knowing he had found spiritual reality and solved the riddle that led back to himself.

Additionally he has learned through all of his inner development, that his current success has nothing to do with other people's lack of it. Everyone is playing out their drama, and his success in no way inhibits anyone else from being successful. Everyone is making up their own game, and he is free to make up his. There is no shortage of energy or resources in the universe. He had chosen and is committed to having this be his breakthrough lifetime. It certainly is and he is elated every day to be here!

There are times when he wants to speak with his personal guides, friends and relatives who are in the spirit world. They are all in the divine love. As he reaches his place of comfort in his meditation, he simply requests his guide(s) to connect with him. He then asks his questions and they reply through soft, gentle words into the inner hearing faculty in the center of his head. Additionally, he sees the message in a vision and hears the empowering words.

The interactive communion meditations have saved him a lot of time and money. For example, there was a house for which he held a second deed of trust. The couple were defaulting on the first and second deed of trust and the house was in foreclosure. He wrestled with buying it back or not. It had liens on it and the real estate market was still depreciating in that area. His guide said, "Do not throw good money after bad." The couple avoided the first foreclosure date by going into bankruptcy. The second foreclosure date was approaching. He would lose his entire second deed of trust at the foreclosure. He waited and resisted becoming a rescuer in this matter. Then a fax came through his machine. The couple had accepted a good offer on the house and it was in escrow. Everyone would end up being taken care of. He did receive payment when the escrow closed. Being patient and relying on the strength of the message, he did not go in and buy the house and just allowed the couple to create into the universe a solution. In time, everyone was taken care of.

When he has used the interactive progression meditation, he has consistently seen himself in a crisp and expensive designer suit by his wife's side, standing in an office space that he owns which is filled with bright light. The energy of the time feels very prosperous, powerful, successful, self-directed, and strong with desirable surroundings. His latest use of Oracle Teaching number five, the progression meditation, shows his business doubling again in the next 10 months. This gives him the confidence that he is continuing to move in the right direction in his life and in his work. So much so, he has hired staff.

The Oracle Teachings' basic principles for purification will propel you into divine love consciousness. May this man's personal sharing of his experiences assist in your self-trust to venture deeply into your self-discovery. May this sharing give you the incentive to meditate and receive the results that the divine love will bring through your gain of soul over mind.

Soul   Remembrance

Female,   Age   46

Major learnings and multiple lifetime reviews in one long divine love remembrance meditation for this one. Her session lasted approximately two hours. She kept going back and further back, until the big issue was revealed. It was quite worth the effort and intention. There was an issue that she wanted to resolve which had created the reason for the session. For several months she had been attracted to another man, not her husband, and it was disturbing her. She did not act upon the impulse, rather she wanted to get to the bottom of what was driving her in this direction. A wise inquiry to protect herself and her marriage. It was a good marriage of many years, well worth saving.

After a deep communion and bestowal of divine love she tuned into her feelings of yearning and longing and followed her soul's remembrance. She was led back to another time, sobbing on the beach as a young woman in her early 20s. She was crying because her beau was lost to the sea. To discover why he was gone, the inner energy of her search led her to an earlier experience of that time. Her man had been taken by soldiers in a boat and it had sailed away. They had struck her down and taken him. Her beau would not let go of his principles, so they took him away.

Later, she went into the convent, tended the rose garden, grew old and became lonely and sad. When she transitioned, her inner voice said her life purpose was to "learn to love". She realized that she had not furthered her evolution of this purpose. As this remembrance did not fully answer her initial issue, she continued to go further into her soul history to uncover more of her past. She continued to follow the initial yearning energy and her soul led her to a life as a man. He was dirty, ragged and in prison. There were chains on his wrists and a sense of hopelessness. His land had been seized, and even though he fought back hard, it was taken. In prison, he often wished he had done it differently and had hidden away in order to be free. He died in prison. As he transitioned, he learned that "he could still have his dignity". A few months later she regressed into this life again and cleared the harshness away with light and healed the holding of the shackles. Still, these were not the main causal experiences of her issue, just parts of the puzzle. She pressed on.

The next remembrance was even further back in her history. She was a teenager, perhaps Greek, and high spirited. She was hiding behind a tree watching a men's council. Because only men were allowed she was forbidden to be a part of it, although she desperately wanted to be. An older woman came by and pulled at her to leave and be safe.

Her father was powerful and wealthy, her mother weak. She was forced to marry an older man who was abusive and mean. She left by escaping to live with friends far away. Again, she died alone and yearning. A pattern is now appearing in her existence's. Why suffering, loneliness and misery?

Committed to resolving her pattern, she continued into her soul history. Next, she found herself inside a temple, rich in earth colors. There were small niches in the walls with candles, labyrinths and nooks. It was a very large Egyptian temple. She was a high priestess performing sacred rituals. Still there was the inner yearning for something else. Surprisingly, she actually did not want to be in the temple. She yearned for having a family, friends and outside life. She wanted a life with a husband and children. This added to the pattern of her lives of feeling incomplete, unaccomplished and left with yearning.

Continuing back further her soul brought her awareness into a life as a young man who was hunting cave man style. His wife died in childbirth and he was very angry. He shook his fist at the sky. Later, as he was climbing down a steep canyon, he slipped, fell and was dashed into the rocks below. He died feeling "abandoned". Another important piece to her puzzle, abandonment.

With a sincere and determined effort, she asked to reach deep inside her memory and to be taken to her main causal experience that was driving all of these lives of unfulfillment. She was successful. She went back, back guided by divine love to her time of formlessness. Her beginning of being in the light and with the divine spirits of angelic love and being. She was ecstatic, sensing the beauty of this existence. Then, she was shown what happened. She started to feel she was falling, falling and falling down back into form for the first time. She felt pushed and that she did not want to go into form. Her spirit guides told her that she needed to go to share love, to share light and to teach. She felt reluctant and fearful.

Then in a dark eerie scene, she found herself in another incarnation being a virgin sacrificed into a volcano. It was a torturously painful experience. Her inner voice was saying, "I don't want to be here. I want to go home, back to the spirit life." Not surprising that she was chosen as the virgin sacrifice. In the perfect balance of the universe, the tribe wanted someone to sacrifice and she really wanted to leave. She created a way out for herself.

She definitely felt her stress release. She was transformed after this divine love meditation and these soul remembrances. She learned a lot about herself in less than two hours. Her future lives were miserable because she did not want to be here and she felt abandoned by her spirit guides. She wanted to show what a lousy time she was having. All of the difficult experiences were only reflections of her disempowering concepts. Now that the false distinctions were unveiled she could digest and decide to be here. Once she claims ownership of the wonderful possibility of being a human in form, her life will soar! The simple formula is to design a life of what you truly want to experience, not to design something terrible that makes you suffer just to show your guides or your parents that you don't want to be here and they are wrong. You are here, so choose to be here. It is your best choice to choose life!

Soul   Remembrance

Female,   Age   50

In her own words, "The Divine Love Meditation has been extraordinarily helpful. It puts me right back in a state of grace, experiencing and expressing from the Spirit that I am. I am inviting in the Divine Love energy each opportunity I have. It is the key for me to keep moving forward. I find that the simplicity and truth of it is in my knowing."

Before she was able to do the soul remembrance meditations, we had to spend several sessions in receiving the divine love inflow. Her spirit body had a few disconnected and restricted areas that were blocking the flow of universal energy to her soul, therefore limiting its size and connectedness. Gently, as each gap was seen in her aura, the divine love and her own inner will to become whole reconnected and expanded the areas into their pure and natural state of wholeness. The divine energy could then be felt more strongly, and the results of her meditations would be more easily obtained. There were recurring common themes in her soul remembrances. Three of the best examples are generously shared.

She is being killed. She is a man in King Arthur's time. He has been betrayed and not understood for who he was and what he believed in. He is on a white horse in full armor, with weapons, in battle with one other man. He is fighting for a cause, feeling happy, righteous, fully knowing he will win.

Then he is struck down. He is laying on the ground, still alive for a short time, but stunned. Stunned that he could be struck down for his cause that was so worthy. He could not understand or believe he was dying. Why could this happen to him? He was totally baffled! He wasn't done with his work and should not be dying. It was his life commitment, and he should not be dying. When leaving the body, this false inner conclusion is made: "I fight for a cause and die! This is slowing me down now. I am the sacrifice."

Once reviewing these disempowering ideas, she reordered them into empowering statements. "I am now the vehicle, not the sacrifice. It is my choice now to keep strengthening my resolve to commitment. Now it's my choice to live and see it through, knowing this is my truth."

The second common theme involved entitlement. She was guided back to 15th century Southern France. She is a beautiful woman, an aristocrat. She lives in a lovely home environment, wonderful clothes and beautiful body. She is in the garden with a man. She is feeling loved, fulfilled, happy, and ecstatic.

In all ways it was the full experience of having it. She had it all, knew it and lived it. Her conclusion was, "Full entitlement has no limits. I can have what I want because of who I am. Beauty and power entitlement were achieved to fulfill the imbalance of my other lives."

In the final example, she was a young maiden in ancient Kaua'i, Hawai'i. She was living by Barking Sands beach near the mountains. She had very special powers. Her tribe needed to protect her. They took her to the rocks and valleys to hide her. She was found and killed for the knowledge and power that she had and was. All are very sad as they hear her dying words, "I will return to continue my work."

At a young age in her current life, she had an experience

of being powerful and revered. She knows she has returned to assist her people, and it is so strong inside of her. She knows she is home. The life purpose of the latter lifetime was to be in touch with her spiritual power, which is a gentle power others may not understand. It is the inner authority within us all.

The return to her former land is a strong factor for this one. So much so, it can become a tunnel vision and a foundation for purpose that is based in the past. The place and people have changed, while this one is still in the struggle for a more updated self identity and cause. Her future soul remembrances will continue to uncover her inner mystery, leading her to a life of true peace where she is not driven to prove or recover something from the past. She is gaining knowledge and learning more about herself each day with the help of our divine inner light. When she used Oracle Teaching number five, the interactive progression meditation, she could see that she was still in Hawai'i. She was walking on the beach wearing colorful beachwear and feeling happy. This vision will help her to trust herself in getting to that place of peace and fulfillment.

She is still on the journey of self discovery. The divine love is a treasure within and a companion. May we all know this great and wondrous gift of love.

Soul   Remembrance

Female, Age 51

This beautiful and sweet woman was surprised that she had had so many male lifetimes. Five of her main concerns were cleared in one two-hour divine love and soul remembrance meditation. She had claustrophobia, was afraid of the dark, had reoccurring shoulder pain, abandonment issues and wanted to complete with her mother who had passed on 23 years ago. Here are her precious sharings, given as a gift to help humanity accept the tremendous value of divine love meditation.

After receiving deep infusions of divine love golden light into her soul, she learned to use the divine love to enhance and balance her metaphysical faculties. With her inner sight and hearing she saw a large gray field of energy floating over her, and began tracking it back to the place and time when it began. She saw herself as a young boy during the colonial period in England. He was of the royal class, and the poor working class was in revolt. He was captured, and then wrapped and tied in leather onto a table. He was face down. His arms, legs and body were tied down. He could only lift his head up. He was screaming at the workers. His neck was aching from lifting his head to scream. The workers hated him because he was royalty. He was murdered; buried alive in a casket placed in the ground. In the remembrance she could see the dirt being shoveled over the boy's casket.

The main thoughts that were coming through were of great sadness for the child who never got to live and see his joy. He loved the workers and thought they were his friends. He saw them turn on him and kill him. The scene was dark, and he was disappointed that he wasn't acknowledged for who he was. No one came to help. He was an innocent child. They betrayed him.

His life purposes were to bring unity between royalty and the poor, to be heard, not to always be alone to fend for himself, and to be loved. His life learnings were humility and love. At the end of the remembrance she felt his sister's great sadness of being left alone by him and the knowing of the darkness in the coffin. She sent love to the sister in her current consciousness and replaced the hardship of the life with her new awareness that the review provided. Her claustrophobia was based in this experience and now could be fully resolved.

As she moved into the next life, she was a 14 year old boy. He was a young cowboy being asked by his mother to go into the town with a message for his father and to pick up a few supplies. He didn't feel right that day, but went because his mother insisted that the message be delivered.

He was a very sensitive child and loved his horse. He also had a dog. As he was riding to town, the horse stumbled badly, hit a rock and died. His own shoulder was jammed very hard into. It was the same shoulder that was bothering her in this present lifetime.

He didn't want to get another horse and became despondent at school. His teacher tried to get him back into living his life. When he was 16 years old he had a girlfriend who loved him, but he couldn't return her the same love nor the love she deserved, as he was still heart broken over the horse. He felt like he didn't deserve anything good for himself.

The truth of the life came forth next. She saw that the boy did not stick-up for what he thought was right for himself. He could have saved himself and his horse. He had not wanted to go to town that day. He could not let go of the guilt and fear which resulted in the day's happening. As he transitioned, his thoughts were, "I am finished with this life. I didn't say good-bye to my dog who brought me joy. I ignored him. I came and went and didn't do anything." After he had fully transitioned and had later met with his guardians, he was asked if he had learned anything. He replied, "I learned love in that life. Love for my horse, for myself and how important it is. I forgot that. I did not forgive myself and still blamed myself for going to town."

She sent love to the girlfriend of that life, the dog and the horse. Her shoulder pain started to go away. It didn't completely disappear, so we began tracking the shoulder discomfort to the next soul remembrance to be reviewed. She saw herself as a male soldier for the British military. He was of slight build, riding a horse at midnight with other soldiers. All of a sudden, a cannon appeared and exploded in the middle of the road. They were being ambushed from each side. The opposing soldiers had been hiding in the forest. A very large soldier from the enemy leaped at him, jamming his shoulder and delivering fatal blows. Of course, this was the same shoulder that was still holding pain in her current body. He transitioned with these thoughts, "It feels better up here. Where I am now is where I am supposed to be in the first place. I am not an aggressive man. I don't want to have anything to do with killing anyone." His life purpose was, "To simply be an Englishman, just one of the many." He learned that, "It was just as easy to release myself up to God as having to give up the country to the opposing soldiers. It was just as easy to let go and give up to God." Additionally, "I learned the contrast of darkness and light. Going to the light feels wonderful. Dark represents killing, death and fear." He could see his girlfriend putting flowers on his grave. As he hovered in spirit over her, he told her everything was all right and patted her on the shoulder. She saw him in his spirit form and was satisfied. He felt good that he was able to give her the knowing of the afterlife.

Now we know where the fear of darkness was coming from. At his guardian review he was angry for having so many lives that ended so soon. He felt guilt for having the anger, and cleared it away with love. Notice that she has had a breakthrough already, at 51 years old in her current life. Within an hour after the session, she said the pain in her shoulder had gone away.

The peak experience in the meditation was the reconnection to her mother who had passed away when she was 28 years old. As I asked her mother to join us, she could see her come close by with a gray field in front of her. I asked her to ask her mother to walk around the field and appear clearly for her to see. She did so. They reunited in their love for each other. They forgave each other of the past and her mother was able to explain why she transitioned early and had kept her from her father. As it turned out, her mother was protecting her from the mental abuse that her father would have treated her with. This made sense to her, as she knew something had been going on. She loved being with her mother again, even though in spirit, and looks forward to continuing to see her in future interactive communions. She felt loved, renewed and acknowledged in her divine love meditation session. She loved the Oracle Teachings and being reconnected with the divine holy light. When we spoke a few days later she was planning to clear more of her past and evolve fully.

You create many blessings for yourself with divine love and by freeing yourself of the past. Trust your soul to guide you to the perfect experiences for purification and evolution. You will learn to trust yourself in the act of soul communion.

Soul   Remembrance

Female, Age 53

Major breakthroughs for this one. In her first divine love meditation she easily received the bestowal of gold light and regressed into her soul remembrances. She reviewed three past incarnations. The first was as a judge who was crooked because he was mad at the system. He took from the rich and gave to the poor in his rulings, to get back at the corrupt system the rich had created. The second life was as a male slave on a large ship, the third as a woman dying while giving birth to her daughter. The overall realized benefits of the soul remembrance meditation were:

* She began to see auras and spirits very clearly as she consulted her clients.

* She had no fear of dying. We are in this dimension only for a while, and death is perfectly natural.

* She now has an acceptance of just the way things are rather than her past usual drive to change the world.

* She is actively functioning out in the world again and not spending too much time at home alone.

Her second private session took place four months later. It was directed to resolve her issues around prosperity and abundance. She would come close to making a gain in money and then something would always come in to dash or strain her assets. She wanted to end this patterning and clear her past. Again, three past incarnations were recalled easily.

In the first one that came through, she was a female in her 30s wearing peasant type clothing. It was an awful time. There was an invasion and purge. All of her family's belongings, herd, land, property of any kind were taken. They were dispossessed of everything. She died of grief and dispair, wasting away.

The negative distinction she made from the terrible experience was "If you have any money or assets, you will get dispossessed of them. It is useless to own anything as it gets taken away." After the divine love soul remembrance, she cleared this disempowering distinction and retrieved those that empower her. They were:

"Things are not important. You take with you your knowledge and experience made by your choices."

"Possessions are not your real security. Your security is in your abilities."

The second incarnation was as an aristocrat. She saw herself as a male riding a horse. This man was caught up in a pattern of always having the rug pulled out from under him just as things would begin to become okay. Recognizing this is only a symptom lifetime, we moved further back into her soul memory to the causal life.

She was a man again, a highly respected middle aged Regent in Ireland. There was a monarchy. Ireland was at war with England. He fought for his people and thought he had negotiated a good deal for his people. It was more beneficial for England to honor the deal than not.

To his surprise, all his people were killed and he was beheaded. He was tricked into believing they were negotiating in good faith. He believed he could save the people. The negative distinctions that he created during and from the experience were: "The betrayal, deceit, enslavement and murder of my people is very painful.

"You want to believe that you can trust they are acting in good faith and there is basic goodness, and they will negotiate like professionals. It all ends up like a sham.

"How can you have faith in anything when you can't trust anyone?"

She replaced these with empowering distinctions. The new distinctions were: "He did not see the deceit at all. He believed what they said. He felt good about himself and his beliefs as a humble man and sincerely fulfilled his responsibilities as a respected Regent."

"The Irish outnumbered the English but the English had better armor. The Irish did not have a good back-up plan."

"Betrayal was the core issue. He had over-invested in other people and they did not follow through."

At the end of her meditation she could see the past pattern and released it completely and filled herself with divine love light. She is clear she had created the constant stress of up and down finances from the negative distinctions. She will now experience a constant smoothness in her financial matters and move on to a clear embrace of her coming abundance.

I spoke with her four days after this meditation. She said she was feeling terrific. She told me something I did not know. She said that she had always had neck pain in her life. Her neck was always stiff, it would feel tight when she would turn her head and would constantly ache. She said the pain for the first time had completely disappeared and her upper spine had straightened! Do you understand how powerful a result this is? She feels that the resolution of the Regent life residue and the clearing of her death due to beheading has made immediate beneficial changes in her body. Note the neck pain and beheading reflection. In another phone conversation she was bringing in prosperity with a large return on a short term stock purchase. What blessings are received in divine love meditation and our soul remembrances.

May her sharing show how much the past dominates the present. *If you want to make great changes in your life, clear where you have been.* You are in complete control of your destiny. May the divine love meditations bring wellness, honor, truth, love, peace, forgiveness, compassion and prosperity into your life.

Soul   Remembrance

Female, Age 54

After two divorces, this beautiful woman wanted to understand her past so that she could create a new beginning for herself. She had moments of loneliness even during marriage and went through great upsets and anger in each divorce.

In her soul remembrance meditation, she followed the angry and upset energy (identified first as a gray energy field around her heart) back into her soul memory, where sections of several incarnations were reviewed. She had been a beautiful woman of high status in Europe. Her husband was always saying how she did not satisfy his expectations and kept putting her down. She never felt that her needs were being met. She felt angry towards him because she did not like him and felt lonely.

In another life she had been trampled to death by knights on horses. She had been told not to be there, it was a dangerous place. She realized that she had made "bad" choices about where to be in life. One of the knights was her beau. She had ignored his request to not be there.

In the third incarnation scene, she was a single woman. She preferred to live alone and would rather not have a relationship. She actually really hated men. She felt she had more self-confidence without a man around. She wasn't clear about relationships.

We additionally used the teachings to track back into her soul history to see what her prosperity blocks were. She had a symptomatic life of being a greedy judge who took bribes. He did not punish the poor, however, and did take from the rich and have them pay damages to the poor people he was judging. Prior to this life, she tracked back to the causal lifetime that created the greed. She had been a slave and it was a very hard life. She chose to leave her integrity behind and switch over to greed to make a better and more comfortable slave life for herself. She felt her survival was based upon "joining" the bad masters.

At the end of her review, she received a beautiful message from her divine love guide. Her purpose this lifetime is to develop the ability to make better choices for herself, realign with integrity, and to choose a partner who truly loves her and who will treat her with love. The divine love meditation and use of the teachings took less than an hour. She was able to release three blocks and replace them with a new direction in alignment with universal law and love. Her life will now change and be a new reflection of wholeness and wellness.

A few months later, we spoke on the telephone. She realized that in her two marriages of this lifetime, she had been a satellite around the men in her life. The meditation helped her to shift and transform herself by releasing her hatred toward men. She is now living her life based on her own needs and desires as her centerpoint. She is developing her new career as a portrait artist and loves it! She moved back to her home country and town where she is close to friends, relatives and her children. She has lost weight, has a new hairstyle, is playing tennis and is taking new risks.

GLIMPSES

Wherever you are on your inner journey, it is helpful to see what others have experienced. It will give you more confidence to trust yourself to go inward. The following are glimpses into a few more meditations to help you further understand how rapid and how potent the results often are.

Let me personally share three such divine love messages I received in 1995.

June 4, 1995: In a vision I saw myself standing in front of a large door made of light surrounded by light. It had no lock. I was deciding whether to push it open a little. All of a sudden the door flew open, then disappeared. A sudden amazing whoosh of my soul's light field fully released from my chest and encircled the earth. It was a profound energy release. I was a global personality from that point on and knew it was time to publish my first book, *The Oracle Speaks: Breakthroughs for Humanity.* I know that I am a universal being and that it was time to participate on a global level with humanity. The final message was, "All the doors are open." It was loud and clear.

June 9, 1995: "Make your presence known!" This message was extremely strong and propelled me into moving forward with sharing the teachings of divine love. It is such a powerful feeling to know that the universal ones support your self-expression and knowledge.

June 15, 1995: "Radiate your light!" Again I received a strong sensation and message making sure that I move forward with my outward communication and mentoring. I was confident that the timing was perfect for modern wisdom and divine love consciousness to become known in a simple format.

In the following months it was a red carpet ride and still is. The doors are truly open. The responses to the divine love teachings touch my heart. Thank you to everyone.

The following are several glimpses from very wonderful people who wish to share their divine love experiences. Each has a different journey, learning and triumphant outcome.

This is a glimpse of a personal sharing from a woman of 60 years of age who was recently divorced. She wanted her story to be told in her own words.

"My experience with The Oracle's past life regression work brought me to an understanding of my life sequences, and of how I came to develop certain aspects. As The Oracle showed me, I glimpsed remembrances that involved being threatened, harmed or put to death on The Trail of Tears. As a psychic in Early American days, I was hunted down in the woods and executed as a 'witch'. As an Egyptian youth, I was somehow silenced for speaking wisdom. There were other more rapid regressions, rather like going backward through a tunnel, until I got to the beginning. As a light energy, spinning off from the oneness on my way to inhabit human form, I saw that I had taken into my field a bit of darkness - just to see 'what could happen'. And so ensued many 'missions on the dark side'.

"Right at this point of recognition of why I had successively evolved with this life pattern of creating traumatic dramas, I was able to choose being energetically a field of pure light. Begone dark spot! Out of fear, during my present lifetime I have often 'stuffed' my truth. No more will I do that. I feel empowered to speak from spirit and from my place of clarity. I am eternally grateful to The Oracle's gentle, yet insistent, loving guidance in achieving this profound healing. She is clearly extraordinarily gifted.

"My awareness of divine love increased over the next several months, and I have continued to grow daily in that consciousness. It has aided me in my journey back into the oneness."

This dear being is now living in her most favorite home. Following her vision to serve love and pursue her true purpose, she is beginning a new business based on love principles. She is able to take her stands, set her boundaries with others, and say no when necessary. Her self-esteem is blossoming and the rewards and riches of the universe are in her hands. She feels the divine love all around her which shines through her eyes and smiles. She looks 15 years younger now.

Here is another glimpse into divine love meditation. I want to share another woman's first soul remembrance as it lifts the fear of dying. In her own poetic words, "It was easy to follow Oracle's soft, resonate voice into the soul's shadowy haze, guiding my mind's eye over my body and inside to find the places that are colored gray, sometimes black or red. When I stop to visit each place colored, blocked, images begin to form: a young woman, giving birth to a daughter. I am very weak, it has been a long and difficult labor. I am dying as the baby is born. I find myself thinking, there is no difference between life and death, both offer an openness to discovery and a trust in movement that was not intended or even expected. Since my experience with Oracle, I am more alert and continuously receiving guidance with more clarity and definition."

Another glimpse was written so beautifully that I want to share it with you just as the gracious woman wrote it.

"I took the divine love course and something happened to my heart. It softened and opened, and I was able to be loving and yet be safe in the world. My own personal day to day experiences became more joyful.

"Then I had the good fortune to do bodywork on Oracle. As a massage therapist I have been fortunate to do the work I love. But when I worked on Oracle my heart filled with golden light. I honestly was so overwhelmed with her heart energy that I was knocked off my feet and I landed on the floor where I sat receiving what I must call a blessing. At my next massage appointment I was with an older woman I had previously worked on I was able to further straighten her curved spine from the intense divine energy that was in my body and my hands. I could see the transformation before my eyes. I measured the woman afterwards and she had become taller and straighter!

"Being with Oracle is fun, and yet I know I am in the presence of a master. Everything around her is light and golden and peaceful.

"I know at this time that her energy is changing. It's as though she isn't solid. She's vibrating so fast and her throat chakra is so huge. I know her message to the world has to be heard. Oracle to me is the divine goddess."

Although her message speaks of my light, her life has unfolded beautifully in the awareness of divine love consciousness. She and her divine complement husband have built their own home and are successful in their work. They are healthy, and their children are grown and out in the world. They have time for their own personal pursuits now, which include the embrace of divine love and living in its light. She is a magnificent massage therapist who is so sensitive she can pick up on anything, no matter how small, that may need to be released from the muscles or accupressure points. We are blessed to know her as well and benefit from her joys and loving touch.

Another glimpse is of a woman in her early forties who would come for meditation intensives every three years or so. She was resistant to surrender her mind to her soul. I kept presenting the light from my core center to redirect her to her soul and to answer her many questions. A long while after I last saw her she sent a loving letter. She had traveled to Europe and India and wanted to see me again. Through all of her travels and the gurus she met, the predominant and pure messages would always come simply from the divine love universe. The power of the divine love overrides all false directions and saves years of struggle and searching and the expense of traveling to others when the truth is always with you.

Let me briefly share another glimpse. This woman was about 46 years old and had been wrestling with cancer off and on over a five year period. She only had time for two appointments when I saw her eight months before she transitioned. Her soul remembrances were all very hard, sad and down-trodden as a female. It was no wonder that she physically looked like a boy in her current life. She didn't want to be a woman. She was very thin and straight with very short hair and no make-up. She wore sport clothing and was tom-boyish. As she began to see her pattern of not accepting her womanhood and goddess aspects she started to recover. However, she was unable to continue her meditations upon returning to her home environment and family as they created an overwhelming masculine environment for her. Her challenge was to accept her femininity and to express her goddess. She was a beautiful person who was very kind and served others needs before her own. When she communicated telepathically to me a week after her transition, she said she had failed to meet her life purpose and goals. She was working on herself further in the light and creating a better plan to achieve her learnings in her next incarnation. People do not always maximize their time on earth; in fact, most minimize it.

One more glimpse is of a man in his 60s. He and his wife flew to Beverly Hills from Florida to see a medical doctor regarding his lingering illness identified as Parkinson's disease. The doctor gave him several tests for his current agility, strength and physical comprehension. I was then given the opportunity to teach him how to meditate with creative visualization. During his second meditation the constant shaking of his head, shoulder and arm completely stopped. He was in slight shock and almost afraid that it might start again. The doctor re-tested and the results of course were 180 degrees different. In the second meditation, the electrical impulses of the occipital area of the brain was reactivated and began sending the natural impulses to that area of the brain which in turn signaled the release of certain chemicals that usually naturally flow and secrete. The Parkinson's disease was arrested. The experience that had caused the illness came about from his tour of duty in the 1940s in Europe. He was separated from his wife, did not care for the military life, and had fallen and broken his arm. He held his sadness and separation emotions in his body. Twenty years later Parkinson's disease appeared. After the simple release of the causal experience he was immediately restored to health. Meditation and the use of our metaphysical faculties are great contributors to living in fullness, wholeness and healthiness.

The most common limitations are past experiences of fear, suppression, control, being killed and tortured. The domination of women and children is very predominant. Prejudice, slavery, greed and not wanting to be incarnated seem to be very repetitive cycles. May these glimpses empower you to take a good look at your past and erase any limiting ideas for unlimited ones of love, freedom and your own truth. *I bless your journey and the final outcome of divinity.*

Your divine soul remembers all of you. Isn't it time to reconnect and find out who and what you really are?

Many have recalled a few past experiences and only hold them as such because they did not thoroughly cleanse the past. The empowerment of the soul remembrances is based on doing them well. It is imperative with each regression to authentically answer the following important questions in order to completely free yourself:

1. What was my life purpose?

2. What were my life learnings?

3. How did I do?

4. Is this experience symptomatic or the

causal life?

5. What is/are the foundational false

distinction(s) causing these experiences?

6. What is the jewel of wisdom gained after

letting go of the false distinction(s)?

You will be surprised and amazed with the misconceptions you created and have carried through time. May you succeed and excel as these people have.

The divine universe will dance with you anytime. There is no one to blame for your life experiences. You are the architect for all that you see, hear, feel and do. Perhaps there are false distinctions in your soul history. May you find the inner resources, by using the Oracle Teachings, to bring you into the awareness of their existence and to receive purification with divine love. You will know when you are succeeding as the world will immediately begin to reflect the improvements. It is a major upliftment to erase false distinctions and replace them with universal knowledge and wisdom. *We are examples of our abilities and of our credibility.* May you always shine brighter and brighter as you descend into your full history. My joy is in seeing you in joyful states of consciousness. The journey need not be long or arduous. It is up to you.

There are very large numbers of people who have begun working with the Oracle Teachings. You may enjoy my new meditation series, "Meditate With The Oracle", as a companion to The Oracle Series of books. Sacred harp music was created to enhance the meditations by a celestial harpist. The cassettes contain four half-hour divine love meditations which will help enhance your communions and carry you into the light and deeper into your soul. Your advancing evolution is a gift to us all.

Allow your natural gifts to be expressed.

You will know yourself in the actions they direct.

ORACLE

CHAPTER FIVE

GETTING STARTED

When you begin meditating and experiencing your soul remembrances or progressions, you may have questions about how to proceed. This chapter addresses the most commonly asked questions about getting started. May it be helpful and assist in your ability to evolve, and may it empower your relationship with your soul, the divine light and the universe. *Soul over mind mastery is your destiny. Once you fully achieve the state of advanced enlightenment you will have achieved your destiny.*

I am afraid to meditate or see my guides. Is this unusual?

It is not only fear that evokes this behavior. It is the unfamiliarity with meditation and the inexperience of having a conscious relationship with your guides that makes one timid. With practice, like learning to ride a bike, you will develop your skill in meditation and your communications with your guides will be clearer, stronger and more frequent.

Allow yourself to gain the wisdom of your inner messages along with the peacefulness and wellness that meditation provides, rather than dwell in stages of tentativeness and shyness. You will gain the grace of the universe and release the ignorance of the mind.

Begin your journey of self-awareness. You will be blessed and caressed by the divine love and its golden light.

I can see the light. How can I become one with it?

With a sincere request, ask the divine love golden light to softly flow into your soul. Ask for golden light, as it is more potent than white light. Continue to ask for the inflow and you will see it coming through your crown and into your energy body in gentle thick waves.

You will notice with each wave that your soul expands larger and brighter. Keep your soul reservoir full by consistently taking the time to receive the bestowals throughout your day. You will notice how smooth and easy life becomes as you learn to walk with the light.

How do I know it's actually my guardian or who my guardian really is?

When you are in your sacred sanctuary during your meditation, ask for your divine love guardian (angel, master, teacher, saint, guide, Christ being, etc.) to appear and join you. As you sense their connection, you will know deep inside who it is and often recognize their face or energy. Ask for their name so you can call for her or him or them in the future.

As you commune with your guardian, feel free to ask any question you want. Leave time for her or him or them to share other knowledge and wisdom with you as well. They have a larger picture, and can assist you in many ways.

You have known them before and they are very close to you. Know that they always have your best interests at heart and that they operate from divine principles.

How do I interpret what I am seeing?

The visuals vary by individual, based upon what system of interpretation works easiest for the person. Some prefer symbols or colors, others prefer plain reality. Choose a positive interpretation as often as you can.

To clearly set the stage, state what type of visions you would prefer to receive with your inner sight. For example the brighter a being's light field, the more evolved they are, or the use of red roses to symbolize a loving relationship versus yellow roses to symbolize a new friendship. Some people prefer words seen as white letters across a blue sky in their visions and just read their messages. Others prefer to hear their messages as soft words coming into the center of their heads. The universe will gladly accommodate your request, or you may just automatically start with a certain form that is natural to you. I advise the less interpretation, the better, so mistakes are less likely to occur when deciphering the symbols.

I operate with reality sight and hearing. I see energy, love, light, beings and things very clearly as they are. I also feel and sense their holiness or negative emotions. I can look further to see where the emotions are coming from in their past and when the truth is being told.

Your communication methods can change through the years. It doesn't matter. What matters is clearly receiving the message and its benefits. Be careful as you add your meanings to the interpretations not to justify or rationalize toward a particular outcome. Discern your messages well and understand them for what they are, as they are. You will excel in your progression to live as a divine being of light.

Do I have to meditate every day or twice a day?

The universe and divine light ask nothing of you. In the beginning you may want to meditate on a scheduled basis to help develop your acumen. After a while you can consciously tune in easily and quickly with your eyes open or closed. Meditate as often and for as long or short of a time period as you wish. Be sincere with yourself and your meditation will be full of new ideas, knowledge and clarity. You will shed your past for a new life based on the real you. *There is no structure for evolution, only your will and desire to reclaim your spirituality and self-determined reality.*

What is the best position or posture for meditation?

I have only one suggestion; do not fall asleep. Sleeping does not create a transformative meditation, although it can create transformative dreams.

It does not matter what position or posture you body is in. Choose comfort and what suits your lifestyle to create a relaxed state of being. You can meditate anywhere at any time. Do not let certain misconceptions about the "shoulds" of meditation, that have been handed down through the millennia, limit your inner communion. Follow your needs and requirements and your meditations will propel you into divinity.

I keep falling asleep and can't meditate. What should I do?

Get some rest, dear one. Your physical needs are a priority. When you find you are rested, then begin your meditation. Meditating in the morning when you first awaken may help you get started. Your day will fall into place nicely and run smoother as you tap into your soul early.

Perhaps later in the day, take a break from the outer world and contemplate the inner world in a moment of silence and soul attention. You will gain energy as you meditate more often, and you will find that you have stopped falling asleep during your evening meditations.

I can't seem to concentrate. My mind keeps wandering or chattering. Help!

There are many reasons for interference with your concentration or relaxation. Sometimes you have not completed something that needs to be done before you meditate. Sometimes your body needs physical exercise to balance your system. Sometimes you do not have enough time to have a good meditation and you are not really present for one. Sometimes your meditation is to be with the wandering and the chattering and to see or hear what needs to be seen and heard. Meditation is not a search for silence or emptiness. Meditation is an experience to listen, hear, feel and sense yourself, your soul, your guardians, the divine love light, the universe, and the pure wisdom and knowledge all of this brings. Relax and receive your meditation experience, and expect it to be different almost every time.

Your other option is, no matter what the apparent reason for being unable to meditate, to know that this is normal for everyone in the early and mid stages of learning and will happen occasionally. Take it in stride and start to meditate again later when your next opportunity arises.

Does it have to be quiet for the most beneficial meditation?

Especially at the beginning, the environment needs to suit your needs. When I began meditation I preferred that it be very quiet. Now it does not matter unless the sounds are so extremely loud they are interfering with my space. You will eventually reach a point in your evolution when you are in meditation all of the time. It is natural for divine consciousness to be fully integrated and an integral part of yourself. As you learn to meditate and advance yourself, your environment will become secondary to your ability to be in the state of oneness.

Can I get lost in meditation or go insane?

Without purity one is already lost and insane. There are degrees. As you grow in your self-knowledge, your true identity will emerge. Your sanity will behold your soul as your home in the universe. You can never be lost in your soul.

Humanity, as a whole, is in various stages of insanity. Only holiness and universal principles emit love and fairness. Take the direct path of divine love consciousness and you will not be lost, as you will be held in the loving arms of our universe.

What happens when you meditate with other people? Is it best to meditate alone?

It is best to meditate and commune with the divine love. Secondary is meditating with others as it is just meditating with others. Meditating alone is just meditating alone. Group sharings are enjoyable, supportive and help some to connect easier. Whichever allows for your fulfillment is a viable path.

Early on, I personally preferred to meditate alone as I could concentrate and listen to my soul without any distraction. I would often take notes with my eyes closed, or open them for a moment to make notes. If I needed a glass of water, I could return and reconnect where I left off quite easily. When I met my divine complement we would meditate together for hours in the evening. Sometimes we would be silent and sometimes we would share as we gained our insights and revelations. I am in a state of meditation all the time now, and during the day I "tune-in" to my soul regarding certain subjects, or beings for more knowledge or to commune with the divine love. In addition, I lead many group meditations and concentrate on being of service to the individuals of the group. I often receive messages for them while in their presence and share the wisdom at the end of the meditation.

What if I don't believe in past lives, multiple incarnations or hypnotherapy?

You are free to believe what you wish. The universal principles covering these processes will not be limited by your beliefs. What is empowering are the tremendous results derived from using the soul remembrance teaching. Regardless whether you believe or do not believe in past experiences or hypnotherapy, the positive transformations will speak for themselves. A person with whom I shared the Oracle Teachings quite successfully over the course of 10 sessions had massive breakthroughs in his soul remembrances. Immediately in his life, positive evolutionary changes would occur. Afterwards, he said although he did not believe in past lives, he did believe in the power of past life regression. His interpretation is: whether you have actually had past lives or not is less important than freeing yourself from the false distinctions that are woven into the stories and scenes associated with these images and remembrances.

Let's look further into this inquiry. Perhaps some of you may think you are just dreaming? The visions and words you experience in dreams during sleep are very symbolic and shift from one scene to another, often very quickly and without warning. You usually do not know who the other participants are, and yet occasionally you are very clear about their identity.

Soul remembrances are nothing like dreamtime. This rules out the possibility that past lives, multiple incarnations and hypnotherapy are dreams. Soul remembrance is really like watching a video of your past existences in both form and formless states. In fact, it is very beneficial to rewind and fast forward to view only the most important experiences that are needed to clear your personal issues and false distinctions. You are the observer of an internal movie that has been played since your first awareness of consciousness. It is absolutely fascinating to see what you have thought, where you have been, what you were, what you did or did not accomplish, and to experience your retrieval of cultural aspects and true history. Soul remembrance is one of the most rewarding activities that you could ever create for yourself. Trust your inner truth and your own soul to honor you with profound and personal messages that will deliver you into purer states of consciousness.

I can't see or hear anything when I close my eyes. Is something wrong?

When you begin meditation you will want to activate and enhance you metaphysical faculties in order to see, hear and feel your soul, your guardians and the divine love universe. After you feel relaxed and ready to begin, ask for the golden divine love light to begin flowing softly into your crown at the top of the head. Receive the divine light into your head. Direct the golden light, by inner speaking, to shine brightly and strongly from inside your brain. Ask it to flow out your third eye (aka single eye) between the eyebrows and also out the back of the head, at the area of the fourth eye (aka occipital area). Ask the light to clear and widen the connecting pathways between the crown gateway and these powerful centers. Continue the downward flow of golden light and embrace your throat, thymus and finally a full infusion to the soul center at the heart. Receive the loving light (unity consciousness, holy spirit, God, divine love, etc.) into your soul and regain your spiritual heritage.

I have recorded four 30 minute meditations on cassette with beautiful sacred music, called Meditate With The Oracle, so that you can join me first hand in divine love meditation. Remember, it was never meant to be difficult to communicate with the divine love and to be a sacred child of the universe. Some people connect quickly, and others need a little longer to receive the divine light. Know that you have the right to live in divinity and oneness. Begin your meditations with the inflow and caress of the divine love golden light and feel the wondrous vibration of our universe.

What if I don't trust what I am seeing and hearing?

After your first meditations, begin making notes in a journal and review them after a certain period of time, let's say a week or two. Keep the messages in order by source: your soul, your guardian or guardians or the divine love light. What are the prevailing messages? Are there similarities in the messages? Is any source more consistent or sensible than another? What you will begin to see is the truth in your communications as well as any untruth or unclear messages. In a future meditation, ask for the unclear message or messages to be made clearer for you. Take your notes again. Over the years you will see the true meaning of some of the insights and knowledge you were receiving for yourself. You will develop your meditation skills and transcend the trust issue as you grow in your self trust. Once you trust yourself, you will then be able to distinguish authentic messages from the soul versus inauthentic ones born of a tricky, fear-based mind.

Can you really talk to your loved ones on the other side?

There are no communication limitations in meditation nor for an adept whose faculties are finely tuned and developed. You can ask to speak with your loved one just as you ask to speak to your guardian or the divine love light. Ask with love for permission to connect with the one you wish to be with and you will speak and be spoken to. All consciousness is holographically in oneness and therefore can be accessed instantly and with ease.

I know many people who now have closer relationships in meditation with their loved ones who have transitioned, than when they were in embodiment. It is never too late to communicate and share your love.

Should I teach my children to meditate?

There are no shoulds in life. You may joyously teach your children to meditate and bless them with the timeless renewed connection to their soul, their guardians and the divine love universe. Your children will be able to access consciousness in its wholeness, rather than live in the limitation of separated mind and ego.

You will find that children are often eager to use all of their abilities, raised in a household that cares for the soul as well as the temporary mind. Give them the gift of inner communion and you will feel that in addition to having their bodies, you will have birthed their souls as well.

I was taught to pray. Can I still pray or integrate prayer with meditation?

It is not for me to decide what you want to do. Learn to meditate well and you will know if it integrates prayer or if it exceeds prayer. The outcome of communion concerns me more than the method of choice. There are styles that are more effective than others. Use your discernment to select or design the most beneficial one for yourself. Remember, the power is based in the sincerity of the communication. I personally prefer interactive meditation as it answers and informs your requests by immediate response.

Sometimes I just can't find the time to meditate. What do you recommend?

If you are a disciplined person, follow your inner clock and meditate well when you do. Don't meditate when you don't want to or do not have the energy to make the time to. Know that the most important result of meditation is the quality of the meditation and not the frequency. Relieve yourself of any burden of time and pressure to meditate and know that meditation is a precious time to enter states of purity and self-realization. You are always loved and blessed whether you are meditating or not. Life, in itself, is a meditation.

Learn to focus all activities on the activity which you are performing. Drive while driving. Work while working. Golf while golfing. Paint while painting. Meditate while meditating. Free yourself from dogma and rituals so that you may experience direct focus and the quality of your endeavor on a singular basis. Your meditations will then become stronger, clearer and more result oriented.

Would a mantra or chanting help me in meditation?

Personally, I feel that any activity which occupies the mind holds you in the realms of the mind. Why do something that circumvents your direct access and relationship with your soul? Is this another reason why humanity has been blocked from enlightenment? Has too much attention been placed on repeated words rather than the authentic individual soul communion that is the direct path of interactive communication and awareness? *Enjoy the riches of your inner speaking and the sacred soft words of the universe.* Mantras and chanting are outdated, and were introduced to occupy the masses. Although they may make you feel temporarily good, they do not bring one into enlightenment. *Do not settle for small exercises. Sit in the lap of divine love consciousness instead.*

Do you reach a point of being completely filled with golden light?

Yes.

Why do people of different backgrounds experience the same light?

Divine love is divine love. Light is light. Holiness is holiness. Joy is joy. What is, is. The universe is in the state of is. Is is love and the ecstasy of love. We are all the same: soul beings. It is only our casing or shell and the languages we speak that look and sound different. The energy bodies of our spirits are the same and are treated the same by the divine love. You are unique by your character and personality. You are unified by your soul and its love.

Why do people of different backgrounds receive different images and messages?

Different images and messages are received so that you do not have to require the services of an interpreter. Who could interpret anyway, as everyone has their own levels of communication and comprehension? The universe provides the translation to each individual. Your direct link to universal divine love consciousness operates this way so that you can receive and send your messages clearly and quickly. A Catholic may see Mother Mary as their teacher, and a Buddhist may see Buddha as their teacher. Neither teacher is better than the other when instructing and guiding with love. *The teacher is not where to place the emphasis, although most cultures have.* The emphasis is best placed upon the teaching and upon focusing your learning to assimilate the truth, love and light. Be not distracted by the form or by the differences in the forms that others use and by which they receive. *Be attracted only to that which guides and guards your destiny into divinity.*

Can you meditate too much?

Eventually one arrives at the advanced stage of supreme consciousness and lives in the state of meditation all the time. However, when you are in meditation all the time there no longer lives the distinction of being in meditation or non-meditation. You will lose the contrast of being in meditation or not being in meditation and you will function in spiritual consciousness naturally and always. In the full state of oneness, you are fully blossomed and there is nowhere to go to or come from, as you are living wholly in the eternal present. My answer to your question is, no.

However, in your early stages of meditation, if you are meditating in a way that creates an imbalance or irresponsible behavior, then I must say return to a less time consuming level or form of meditation. You can meditate your life away (and I have seen people do this) when on the spiritual path while ignoring the necessary care for yourself, family, home, employment, nutrition, exercise, etc. My answer to your question is, yes.

What if your family and friends do not want to learn to meditate?

Mentor your results and cherish your new found inner joys and freedom. You are responsible for your life and are the ultimate guardian for your soul, as they are for theirs. Focus on your own development and share your love, forgiveness and listening skills with them. You will improve the dynamics of your relationships, independently of their behavior. Live and walk in your sacred awareness and see their natural light and potential. Remember, that you were once without meditation, too. Also, remember, that some do not need meditation. Some are serving from the heart already, and you may be seeing them for the first time.

How soon will I notice changes in my life from meditation?

True meditation grants immediate peace, love and wisdom. The universe will reflect the evolutionary advances of the being within hours, days, or sometimes weeks, depending on the area that is shifting. Pay attention to the evolution, and the effects you desire will naturally follow. Don't focus as much on the results, but use the results as feedback from the universe, measuring your effectiveness. Focus on your inner growth and new actions to continually create the results you truly want.

Will meditation improve my health?

The learnings derived from meditation and the infusions of divine love energy will be reflected in your life, including your physical body. Reconnecting with your soul and obtaining the knowledge that will heal you, will definitely improve your mental, emotional and physical health as your thoughts create and encompass the entire you.

Please note that there are limits to improvement of health if one is too far down the path of illness. You can place yourself beyond the point of return, and begin working with the physical body too late. Your body will always give you warning signals in the early stages of illness. Do not ignore these signs that are for you to see and respond to.

Why do some religions not use meditation?

There are three main reasons: one, the leaders do not know how; or two, it is kept from the congregation; or three, they wish to use something else. Meditation is being recognized more and more and will be relied upon by people of all backgrounds. Concentrate on your development and do not preoccupy your thoughts with what some other religions may or may not be doing. The power is in your conscious awareness of your own identity and the recognition of the wisdom within you.

Is meditation different for women than men?

No.

Can you see God in meditation?

The divine love light is the presentation and entity that many have named God. Yes, you do see God and sense the profound love that emits from the universal energy.

A better question to ask is: Do you see the light within you in meditation? The answer is yes, and you can see it glow brighter and brighter! *You know what this means about who you are, don't you?*

Some of the getting started questions are simple ones. They are meant to assist those who find meditation or the Oracle Teachings as new subjects. For the advanced meditator, I would like to express that you have the developed experience to retrieve your answers directly. Use the teachings and evolve.

The insights that are realized during meditation arise from your willingness to allow and pursue the enrichment of your internal awareness. Reality is only a reflection of your inner ideas. With each new insight, new experiences that heighten your well-being, abundance, pleasure, comfort, friendship, artistry, etc. are released. You evolve faster using meditation than not. The time made for self-introspection, organization or advancement of evolution allows your soul to teach you. The inner listening and inner sight are your greatest teachers. They are pure and authentic as they exist to transmit divine love.

Soul over mind consciousness grants authentic living.

ORACLE

CHAPTER SIX

AUTHENTIC LIVING

The previous sharings demonstrate how the mind's false ideas control your thoughts and actions by suppressing the beauty and bounty of the soul. You give the mind permission to invent and hold these fantasies over your soul-self. *The hidden secrets of the mind can be found and are the real keys to purification, freedom and enlightenment.* You may have made interpretations and misconceptions that served in your previous incarnation experiences but which now limit your evolution. You may be interested in clearing your past, using the Oracle Teachings to bring in an abundant and joyful present.

Enlightenment is the lifting of the mind's insanity for the reality of the soul. Your soul can provide all and everything for you. The harmony of the universe serves the soul. It is for you to strengthen your inner sight, inner hearing, self-trust and self-esteem. Thus, you will be led into the simple lifestyle of a wise being who is wholly in the present. Living in the now means not living from any negative or false ideas from your past history.

Authentic living is not a voyage or journey to some thing, some state or some place. When you live consciously in the present, you have evolved beyond the negative emotions of the history of your soul's past. As you review your soul history, the Oracle Teachings and your own soul invite you into authentic living. There is no place to go other than to the home of your soul. In this advanced state, or shall we say natural state, your soul overrides the mind.

The soul is your consciousness aligned and embraced fully in the universal divine love light. The soul is pure and holds the profound energy systems and laws by which the universe functions. What I mean by "holds the profound energy systems and laws" is that your soul exists in the is of the universe and innately knows what is. It emanates light and love, and therefore functions within the laws and natural systems of the universe. It is easier to flow with the universe than to submit oneself to false distinctions and symptomatic patterning. You can develop a new matrix for your life purpose and learnings or continue with the ones that were created prior to your incarnation, good or not.

As you clear the past, your matrix automatically re-designs itself into alignment with the universe. *It becomes easier to let go of the self-imposed limitations and embrace the powers of the universe.* Authentic living abides by universal law and principles. It fulfills and nurtures the being to stand tall in the world as a soulful one. *All great philosophers and teachers have unraveled themselves to walk with the sacred light and live in divinity.*

The divine love encourages you to actualize your soul-self. You will then model the pure standards of the universe. You will see and feel the presence of others who have done the same and know that you have achieved your goals. Your energy can be used to benefit the world and supply your worldly needs instead of squandering it on mental and emotional stress and upsets. You will begin to live in a self-created state of "smoothness", where the feedback of people and matter are consistently gentle, supportive and endearing.

THE MASTERY

Authentic living mastery acknowledges that we are all the same. Even though we are gathered together by various circumstances, conditions and choices, we can all vibrate in and breathe universal light. *To behold a reality of oneness, kindness and knowledge and its platform for true creativity is the mastery.*

How are universal qualities obtained and integrated? Through each moment, in the moment, making decisions with integrity, responsibility and discernment. This builds your experience and therefore your status of evolution. You will make your choices and decisions from love and compassion for love and compassion.

There are many major choices facing people in their lives. *Authenticity will prevail only if you can operate from its place of origin in your soul, along with the ability to ascertain true facts in each situation.* If the facts are not all available, use the remote viewing of Oracle Teaching number five, progression meditation, to fill you in with more information. Insights or warnings can be ascertained from Oracle Teaching number two. You can also use this interactive form of communion for helpful messages from the light, your soul or your guides. The telepathic and visual messages will assist you in maintaining your alignment and focus with universal principles and your plans.

The following are a few examples of making authentic living choices. Perhaps there are some areas in your lifestyle that can be reviewed and improved.

Overpopulation:

My divine complement and I have chosen to not have children in order to assist in lowering human over-population and consumption. (Jacques Cousteau states that this is the number one issue for humankind that needs resolution. One western child consumes more than an entire remote tribe! Take the parents of two children occupying the planet *simultaneously* and add to their count of four, the grandparents who had the parents who had the grandchildren. You end up with 6 people using resources and creating refuse. It isn't about having one child to replace yourself on the planet and another to replace your spouse, the simultaneous occupation of the planet is where the stress and imbalance occurs.)

We are clear about our life purpose expression and travel the divine highway of truth sharing our teachings. We are not lonely and do not require a nuclear family. We both felt children would take a considerable amount of time away from our expression and we did not have the dharma (service). This helped to limit the amount of other incoming entanglements that occur with the additional associations that children bring. We are very happy with this choice and how it has kept our lifestyle "simplified". For us, this is an authentic choice for authentic living.

For someone else, having a family is their life purpose and they are true to themselves in doing so. Growth without children and growth with children is reality. It is when having children without the desire, life purpose, responsibility or planetary responsibility that one gets entangled for many years in inauthentic living. It distracts you from your life focus, as you are drained of the necessary energy it takes to focus on your needs. Just because everyone is doing something doesn't mean it is the thing to do. A large percentage of parents are staying together just for the kids. How authentic is this behavior? A larger percentage of parents are now single parents having to raise the child or children alone. How authentic was the partner's original commitment to care for the coming child(ren)? The wise one uses consideration and developed thinking before making major choices. The result is a life in favor of its natural course to divinity rather than a life of obstacles and distractions. Perhaps this example invites you to bring true "thinking" about your situation and lifestyle.

Here are other ideas to contemplate. What do you consider to be the two worst inventions of all time? Stop and think about this for yourself before reading on. Consider the possibility that electricity and the wheel are two of the worst inventions ever created! Or, is this due to humanity's improper use of them? Populations have increased dramatically, either oblivious to or, in fact, due to these inventions. Over-population started in ancient times. Whether or not there were the wise ones to lead and control the tribe with universal standards that would protect and survive the tribe in balance, we don't know.

We do know that population was not controlled. Did humanity ever have an evolved society? If humanity did, why did it lose its hold on sanity and balance? Should it not have if the tribe was collectively wise? Would they have not withstood the tests of time, or did temptation and ego dissipate their wisdom and sacred standards?

Career:

Another example of authentic living is being true to yourself regarding your self-expression in your work. Your employment using your finest and most enjoyed gifts is the actualization of your life purpose, or one of your life purposes. As you may have read in my first book, *The Oracle Speaks*, my life purpose remains the same in each incarnation. I enjoy the spiritual life and modeling of it the most, and therefore teach meditation and live in oneness with the light of our universe. This is authentic living for me.

For some women the executive career is not fulfilling and in meditation they discover having a family is their life purpose. For others being a screenwriter of positive films is their life purpose, but instead they find themselves struggling with current positions as computer programmers, housecleaners, and waiters.

Rediscover yourself and listen within to your soul's pureness and you will hear your inner voice of who you are and how you wish to express yourself in your true work. Take the necessary steps to create a strong foundation upon which to begin your life purpose work, and know the great pleasures of being in alignment with your soul-self.

Listening and Serving:

Another authentic consideration is how you operate in your relationships. Be it family, friends or acquaintances, it is all the same. When they are speaking are you giving them your full listening? Are you too busy preparing your responses to the conversation while they are talking to you? Are you serving their requests or are they having to repeat them to you to see if you heard them? Your actions will improve and the depth and clarity of the relationship will be empowered by 100% by listening and serving. You will be able to move life along and evolve your relationships. Your partners will be satisfied and will learn to listen to you better as you model this authentic behavior.

Take a moment to give your listening to your loved ones today or to your co-workers, and see how amazing the response is. You will give your love and your friendship through patience and attentiveness, both qualities of an advanced soul.

Other subjects to consider and review for yourself, and to see if you are authentically living by your innermost knowing and needs are:

1. Partnering with your soulmate rather than someone who is not the right match for you.

2. Purchasing the most environmentally compatible products.

3. Purchasing products from the most "green" companies.

4. Telling friends, family and others the honest truth at all times. This includes saying "no" when you want to.

5. Keeping your promises or notifying the corresponding parties of any changes.

6. Being a non-violent and non-abusive person towards all species.

7. Being clear of negative emotions.

8. Operating without greed or attachment to money. Using money as a tool and supportive energy for yourself and the global village.

9. Developing compassion and giving from this place.

10. Loving your family and friends.

11. Living a balanced life that includes fun, joyful times, leisure and pleasure.

12. Leaving where you have been in better shape or harmony than when you arrived, if there was room for improvement.

You can think of more areas for authentic living. Some may be small gestures as the following example.

Some people choose not to play the sport of golf. There are two main reasons they choose not to. The golf courses completely change the culture of the third world countries they are in or are being placed into. The chemically maintained courses kill the bugs, the birds and insects ingest the poisons, and the runoff destroys the underground water supply, streams, reefs and coastlines. There may be a few organic courses around. I have heard of only one. It seems, as with other businesses, the owners and management base their decisions primarily or solely on money and have dropped the environment principle from the formula. If you want to play golf it could be a gainful experience for yourself and humanity to ask for the management and ownership to consider going "organic". It will cost less, rekindle the soil of the earth and contribute to saving the environment and your health. Looking the other way would only continue to hand the exponentially degrading world issues and problems to the next generation. Why tolerate what was handed down to you or created by your generation?

For some, authentic living is walking rather than owning and using an automobile. By selecting homes in locations where walking for supplies, exercise and entertainment is convenient, the use of an automobile is unnecessary. An occasional ride with friends or in a taxi probably happens minimally.

Others choose to have a gentle vegan diet to authentically demonstrate peace to other species. Albert Einstein acknowledged the harmonious diet saying, "Nothing will benefit human health and increase the chances for survival of life on earth as much as the evolution to a vegetarian diet." Great thinkers and philosophers develop great compassion which includes a plant-based nutrition program which is authentic and in alignment with universal principles. May humanity join in this basic awareness and benefit from nature's gifts.

Living in direct communication with the divine love and your own soul is as authentic as you can get. Your choices for authentic living are many, and are in front of you to see. Perhaps the above sample portrayals will point you to a new beginning. Let your new inquiries lead you to a gateway for a clearer life of authentic choosing. The mastery is in each moment as you are faced with the constant arrival of daily and hourly points of decision making.

In summation, the Oracle Teachings show the way to the life of masterful living. They are easy. They unveil and expose false premises, erroneous distinctions and misconceptions that have been hidden deep within. You will gain more and more authentic living in all areas of your life as you excel in your purification.

Even though all experiences, good and bad, are self-imposed, you have set yourself up to break through a few hurdles in order to gain something else. There are quite a few people whose life learning is to further develop their inner strength or independence. You are very selective when creating the circumstances you are born into in each incarnation. A controlling parent may give you the opportunity to build your strength to stand up to her or him and change the dynamics. A spouse running off and leaving you with all the bills and the children may give you the opportunity to build your independence. A crooked realtor may give you the opportunity to teach the difference between right and wrong or build your confidence in taking stands against evil. As you increase your competence in authentic soul over mind living, you will increase your enjoyment and pleasure. Learn to nourish yourself by integrating your soul further.

The soul remembrance sharings show how you can reach inside and discard the unworthy ideas of your past. Through your own meditations feel the incentive for living authentically by surrendering to your inner powers and fine gifts. We are all here to be our authentic selves. Finding yourself can be achieved quickly and you can then begin contributing what you dreamed of contributing when you were in the planning stages for this incarnation. Be not dismayed by the way the world is. It is empowering to focus on your needs. You will model and mentor to the world the qualities of the universal soul and its authenticity.

CHAPTER SEVEN

A PERSONAL BLESSING

Since my full mystical enlightenment experience in 1980 I have known the ecstasy of inner bliss, peace and joy. I spent a decade working to create a time when I could provide myself the full time opportunity to unveil completely and embrace divinity. The following six years were spent designing the Oracle Teachings and waiting for the proper time to make the presentation of The Oracle Series. This is my present to you, made with divine love and given with the fullness of my heart's light.

I receive great joy when I hear and see the divine love begin to appear in the gentle ones I meet or receive letters from. My soul flutters in my heart with such delight and dances as the divine love starts to become accepted by humanity. We are reaching a new level of consciousness that no longer will be limited, hindered, or denied self-empowerment and personal direct access to enlightenment and living. The old structures no longer work like they did and people are having to reach deep inside and align once again with the constant and true universal principles and laws. As you reach deep inside to your soul, know that your soul's place is naturally an unbound and free energy field that radiates in your spirit space and place in all that is. The way to self-realization is not through another, any institution or its dogma. You can commune directly from your soul to the universal oversoul of love. It is no longer necessary to be suppressed; it is time to express. I am expressing to you all that I am and have been. I have incarnated into most cultures and their religions and structures. The common basic and repeated truth is always the same; it is up to you to gain wisdom and bond at a core soul level with the divine love. Ultimately perhaps your evolution will not be denied. You will live in purity and bliss.

I will be there with the divine love, and its all-inclusive oneness, to greet you as you enter this profound gateway. It is a phenomenal experience to live in divinity with your soul blossomed, with petals of purity and leaves of simplicity. I welcome you to the sacred garden where souls blossom in the light and are watered with empowering love.

Clear your trail to the gateway and walk into your soul. You will be embraced by the others who have blazed the trail and passed through the gateway, also. We are all blessing each of your golden steps that return you to your pure self.

You will bask in the golden light and enjoy living in serenity and satisfaction. You will walk in your own wisdom and the power of the distinctions that grant divinity. My words are spoken in universal oneness and fulfill my destiny and purpose. May we touch each other's hearts and share our sacred knowledge. I am happy to have connected with you and send you my personal bestowal of golden light and its love. It is all that I have and can truly give you. My love is a part of all there is and I share it with you. You are loved. Allow the universal divine love to love you. Allow your soul to love you. Love yourself and know you are returning home and will see it as if for the first time.

CHAPTER EIGHT

OPEN LETTERS

We are guardians of our own souls.

ORACLE

Dear One,

We have all come to share our love with one another. It is easier to express your love than to suppress it. The resistance to the natural flow of divine and natural love energy is an unbalanced and exhausting exercise.

Your heart calls to be opened further and allowed to outflow the love it wishes to give. Give yourself the permission to take the first steps to gift your love to those that are closest to you. The response will be fulfilling and enlightening and will allow for further exchanges of the love principle and its expression. After all, are you not the vessel of sacred honor to bestow the grace of light upon those with whom you share this existence?

love,
Oracle

Dear One,

The insights that are realized during your meditations arise from your willingness to allow and pursue the enrichment of your internal awareness. Reality is only a reflection of your inner ideas. With each new insight, new experiences that heighten your well-being, abundance, pleasure, comfort, friendship, artistry, and other areas of your life are released.

You evolve faster using divine love meditation than not. The time made for self-introspection, organization or advancement of evolution allows your soul to teach you. The inner listening and sight is your greatest teacher. It is pure and authentic when based in divine love consciousness. You will recognize yourself again as you move further into your own divinity.

Your Oracle

Dear One,

You have come so far to be your soul-self. Know that you are constantly being acknowledged and praised for your advances into purer states of consciousness by your loving spirit guides, teachers, helpers and guardian angels. They are embracing you as you step forward into self-realization.

There are many paths to peace and happiness. Using the inner messages that your soul and your guardians provide, enhances and expedites the process. They also are transmitters and receivers of the divine love.

Reality is filled with love and ecstasy. You, too, can resonate in these vibrations naturally. Your soul will unfold and dance in the light of love, and joyfully release the restrictions of the mind. With love you can process quickly and clearly into joy. Trust your soul and the divine love. I celebrate your growth. Love, Grace

Dear One,

All lessons lead to oneness and love.

Do you not see that your potential is available as an experience in the now? It does not have to be delayed until tomorrow or next year. If you take hold of your destiny there will be none. The same for fate, there will be none. There will just be now.

The universal divine love unites us all in the regiving of kindness and support. The Oracle Teachings define boundaries and clear false distinctions so that you can surpass the mind for the jewels of the soul.

Let your soul expand and radiate its messages of eternal wisdom. You will find that you can relax into who you truly are and be accepted as you are, in this world. The relief and release of the burden of the false self is a great accomplishment, well beyond material satisfaction. You will then be able to carry your enlightened self into your next life and start anew in an advanced state of consciousness.

Complete your current spiritual journey soon and

rejoice in your delights of the universe's alignment. Others will see your progress and want to join you. Enjoy the advances and share your learnings.

Love,
Oracle

Dear One,

It takes courage and forthrightness to persevere through your soul's remembrance and to replace the forgotten limiting ideas with the purity of the soul's desire for this incarnation. Be bold in your self-discovery so that you may unveil your soul fully to yourself. You will bring forth such greatness of clarity and insight, and all of us shall enjoy it.

Support your friends and family as they learn from within as well. We can all mutually support one another with the process of purification and self-love. *Relax into your essence, and become the presence of noble sacred oneness.*   Love, Oracle

Dear One,

Each moment is the moment of itself. Your life is a living awareness from moment to moment. Your life is a collective of the moments and the choices made within their time. Does it not occur to you strange that it is habit not to enjoy each moment and make the best of it?

If you slow your pace, could you give yourself a moment in the realm of fulcrum peacefulness, like the support upon which a lever rests? In this place, you can stop and breathe and relax. In this place you can hear and hold your soul-self within your conscious awareness. This powerful place gives you a constant perspective of what is and how you are.

It is not your purpose to run yourself straight through each day and go to sleep in exhaustion. It is for you to see yourself, your life and interact with love and completeness in each association. Please learn to expand your existence by letting go of the control to perform, for the fulfillment and joy of your beingness is in the present. *love, Oracle*

Dear One,

Do not be enamored, be enlightened. Let your past speak to you freely, as it is the doorway to your purification and newness. Your easiest route for succeeding is within your own being.

Your love will unveil itself as you unveil your soul-self to yourself. Your self-approval and willingness to define new boundaries and to create from self-determination will be the main components of your empowering formula to be partnered with the divine love of the universe.

New perspectives and angles will appear from nothing. Be not surprised and yet be surprised, simultaneously. You are a great wonder of the universe already. I see your wonderfulness wholly and holy as it is. Let us walk together in the loving light that is within and without.

Dear One,

To obtain knowledge is not to acquire information and to press into realms of humanism. *True wisdom is an internal awareness that is derived in many ways, all leading directly to what was and what is and what you already knew.* So, it is not to obtain at all, it is to hear, see and listen once again to the light which is you, and to the universe which is also you. Do you feel the truth in these words or just merely understand them?

Direct experience is to re-experience your original soul-self. That is all. As you lengthen your conscious time in authentic original beingness, you lengthen your existence in the state of divine love consciousness. Instead of re-obtaining yourself, you can re-absorb yourself into the fullness and radiance of the brilliant child of sacred heritage once again.

Remember, when humanity no longer needs commandments spelled out, none will be given. I give you my personal blessings as we grow together in the light.

Dear One,

The mastery is not the achievement; it is the willingness and desire to acquire love, joy, peace, happiness, compassion, fairness, loyalty, kindness, wisdom, truth, discernment, distinctions and divine consciousness. The force that carries you throughout eternity is the bounty of the soul and it is what it brings to yourself and the world. The mastery is only an accumulative outcome of these qualities obtained by your development of will and desire.

By focusing your will and desire to conquer what is not consciously known within you, you will advance your spirituality and model the great light and its love. Learn to grow in your determination and you will have the power and strength to surpass any of the self-imposed obstacles and lessons you have set forth.

Know that we are all alike in our holy spirits, and that we can purify our consciousness with the sweetness of our hearts and the natural presence of our souls. Remember to be your soul-self, and rest in this profound place.

Dear One,

As you can imagine, speaking and teaching from the holiness of the soul is an exquisite feeling. You are operating from your central core and most secure place that is based within. It is the most natural place to be. Come to know this sacred soul place by expanding your moments in your inner sanctuary during your meditations. Then bring them forward into your non-meditation times. Start with five minutes, expand it to 15 minutes, two hours . . . and you will soon find yourself in it or there, all day all the time.

It is a tremendous sensation to walk with the light. You will know this place more and more and see it again over and over. Share this conscious level with your precious ones and know they will be some of the deepest sharings and most everlasting.

Dear One,

We have all come to share our love with one
another. It is easier to express your love than to suppress
it. Resistance to the natural flow of divine and natural
love energy is an unbalanced and exhausting exercise.

Your heart calls to be opened further and allowed
to outflow the love it wishes to give. Give yourself the
permission to take the first steps to gift your love to
those that are closest to you. The response will be
fulfilling and enlightening and will allow for further
exchanges of the love principle and its expression. After
all, are you not the vessel of sacred honor capable of
bestowing the grace of light upon those with whom you
share this existence? *Lovingly, Oracle*

Dear One,

The opportunities in front of you are absolutely tremendous! They are for you to see and make use of. Be still for a moment, enter into your meditation and see one appear clearly for you now.

Receive this great gift and bring it from energy into matter. You will experience the natural formula of the universe assisting you successfully.

Turning energy into matter is not fascinating; it can be simplified and made easy. What is fascinating is the unveiling of new wisdom and its knowledge. Learn to manifest in your divine creative space for fulfillment of your expression and abundance. Always make time for the receiving of your new knowledge and wisdom. Your world will become more joyous and carefree!

love, Oracle

ABOUT THE ORACLE

The search for meaning in a material world has, for many people, uncovered a labyrinth of religions, cults, sects, teachers, gurus, dogma and New Age ideas. In this context, The Oracle Series is a refreshing guide back to Self for the answers to the apparently mystifying questions of our times.

"What is knowledge?" "What are truths?" "What is love?" "What is wisdom?" "Who am I?" "How can enlightenment be achieved?" "Is reincarnation a reality?" These burning questions and many more are addressed with simple, clear language by The Oracle. This is her first book series.

The daughter of "good", middle class Presbyterian Californians, she found herself at the age of 27 living an outwardly successful life. "I had all the material things anyone could want. There was the career, the house, the car, wardrobe - everything seemed great, but I began to feel depressed, lonely and very sad". This is when she asked herself what was missing. As many people are currently asking themselves, the answer was "a sense of knowing God". It was a question that would change The Oracle's life and the lives of those around her.

In February, 1980, The Oracle recalls, her awareness and metaphysical faculties were awakened during her very first meditation. She began to devote more time to the inner life. After three months of pushing and striving to "achieve" enlightenment, she discovered she need only relax and receive the divine love inside rather than use any particular method or "special technique".

On May 5th, 1980, she experienced the dramatic state of enlightenment that Indian, Buddhist and Christian mystics have described throughout the ages. After this breakthrough experience she neither slept nor ate for several weeks. During the next nine years, she continued her spiritual journey with a conjunctive material life which provided the prosperity for establishing a life of full-time spiritual focus.

Her ability to read souls developed into a capacity to see holographically and help people to identify false distinctions that inhibited their inner growth. Through the divine love meditations they began achieving soul over mind consciousness.

Through soul remembrances, The Oracle discovered a personal history of 20 incarnations spent as a spiritual teacher devoted to guiding others to the light of love, truth and wisdom. This series is a natural culmination of 15 years experience of soul development, but it might just as well be described as the result of 21 lifetimes of sincere sharing and teaching. From a place of deep wisdom, The Oracle shares her insights and knowledge and teaches the reader to use timeless, unstructured, yet basic tools to empower and support authenticity.

The essence of The Oracle Series is that ultimate truth, wisdom and freedom are located within the soul of each individual and the discovery of that truth does not rely on any teacher, religion, guru or special ritual or practice. In this message, the books question the assumptions of many New Age and old religious concepts and encourage the spiritual seeker to take full personal responsibility. Although the tone of the new philosophy is soft and gentle, the messenger is firm in her intent to "ground the New Ager and help those with a religious background to open up the soul and receive the light".

We welcome your interest in our other products.

To order, kindly telephone 1-800-842-8338 (USA),
fax 001-810-987-3562 (USA),
E-mail: oracleprod@aol.com or
mail to: Oracle RLS, Box 5030, Port Huron, MI 48061-5030 USA

____*The Oracle Speaks* book, US$12.95 plus US$4.00 shipping
and handling

____*The Oracle Teachings* book, US$14.75 plus US$4.00 s/h

____*The Oracle Speaks* on two audio cassette tapes, 2.5 hours,
US$19.95 plus US$4.00 s/h

____*The Oracle Teachings* on two audio cassette tapes, 2.5 hours,
US$19.75 plus US$4.00 s/h

____*Meditate With The Oracle* - two cassettes of four 30
minute divine love meditations with sacred harp music.
US$19.75 plus US$4.00 s/h

____Please send 8" X 10" signed b/w photograph of The Oracle,
US$16.00 each, includes s/h

____Please add my name to your confidential mailing list

* Please add 6% sales tax for Michigan, USA addresses and 12.5% GST to New Zealand addresses.

** New Zealand and Australian orders please mail to:
Oracle Productions Ltd., P O Box 6146, Wellesley St., Auckland 1036, New Zealand

Name:_____

Address:_____

City:_____State:_____

Zip Code_____Country:_____

Phone:(_____)_____

VISA__ or M/C__ (***additional air mail postage for foreign addresses)

Name on credit card:_____
(please print clearly)
Account No. _____

Exp. Date_____ _____
Authorized Signature